In My Own Words

Words

Living with Traumatic Brain Injury

TED GOODRICH

iUniverse

IN MY OWN WORDS
LIVING WITH TRAUMATIC BRAIN INJURY

Copyright © 2016 Ted Goodrich.

All rights reserved. No part of this book may be used or reproduced by any means, graphic, electronic, or mechanical, including photocopying, recording, taping or by any information storage retrieval system without the written permission of the author except in the case of brief quotations embodied in critical articles and reviews.

iUniverse books may be ordered through booksellers or by contacting:

iUniverse
1663 Liberty Drive
Bloomington, IN 47403
www.iuniverse.com
1-800-Authors (1-800-288-4677)

Because of the dynamic nature of the Internet, any web addresses or links contained in this book may have changed since publication and may no longer be valid. The views expressed in this work are solely those of the author and do not necessarily reflect the views of the publisher, and the publisher hereby disclaims any responsibility for them.

Any people depicted in stock imagery provided by Thinkstock are models, and such images are being used for illustrative purposes only.
Certain stock imagery © Thinkstock.

ISBN: 978-1-5320-0091-1 (sc)
ISBN: 978-1-5320-0094-2 (hc)
ISBN: 978-1-5320-0090-4 (e)

Library of Congress Control Number: 2016911741

Print information available on the last page.

iUniverse rev. date: 08/27/2016

Contents

Part One

Introduction 1

Chapter 1: Achievements, Accomplishments, and Background 5

Chapter 2: The Day That Changed My Life Forever 11

Chapter 3: Being Found: Was It by Chance, or Was It Fate? 14

Chapter 4: Was It Really the Dome Light? 18

Chapter 5: Initial Medical Confirmation 20

Chapter 6: From Bad to Worse 23

Chapter 7: The Night God Took My Hand 26

Chapter 8: A Decision to Make: A Parent's Worst Nightmare 31

Chapter 9: Destination Unknown 44

Chapter 10: Reflection 49

Dedication 65

Part Two

Introduction 71

Chapter 11: The First Day of the Rest of My Life 73

Chapter 12: Extent of My Injuries: The Big Picture 76

Chapter 13: Adjusting to My New Home 82

Chapter 14: Meeting Old Friends as New Friends 86

Chapter 15: My Career: Reality or Fairytale? 104

Chapter 16: Reality Check: A Tough Learning Experience 109

Chapter 17: A Career-Making Decision: Do It Now 114

Chapter 18: Goals Made, Set, and Delivered 121

Chapter 19: Sadness Looms Once Again 133

Chapter 20: Here Come The Rainbows 141

Chapter 21: A Decision to Be Made: Quality of Life 146

Dedication 167

"Couldn't put it down! I remember when this happened and it was great to hear all the details from Teddy's point of view. Seeing all the pictures was a great touch. I'm really looking forward to his next book which continues the story!!"

5.0 out of 5 stars
Cindy Meyer (on Amazon Review)
"Ten Seconds"

Part One

Introduction

Life is the most precious thing that any individual can have. Life is not about what you have, how much you own, or how much money you earn. It is not about all the material things with which someone may surround himself. Life to me is who you are as an individual—your family, the friends you surround yourself with, your faith, your character, and your values. I believe that God is the creator of all things, and he gives us the tools we need to make the life we want for ourselves. I am a man who believes that things happen for a reason, whether it be good in nature or in the form of tragedy. The difference in many cases is how you handle situations, and how you pick yourself up from those tragedies. I had endured such a tragedy at an early stage of my adult life—one that took a very long time to recover and heal from. Some of it will never heal, but this experience has taught me so many lessons about life and myself.

I may have never learned some of these lessons if it were not for this horrific event that happened early in my life. It was a tragedy that, without the divine intervention of God, would have been impossible for me to overcome.

The telling of my story began as a project for myself as a healing method. I sought to write down my thoughts and feelings I was going through at this particular stage of my life. I had to make a dramatic, life-changing course of my livelihood, which was going to affect those closest to me once again. Once I had started writing this, it became much more than that. It took on a life of its own and made me realize how blessed and fortunate I was in recovering from something like this. It also made me think of how much I as an individual took for granted in my everyday activities. As I continued to write down my thoughts, it became evidently clear to me that doing this could conceivably be a benefit to someone who may have experienced a similar trauma. There are various traumas that affect different people in different ways, but one thing they all have in common is that it takes personal strength, self-motivation, tremendous family support, and a true belief in faith to get through them.

I wrote my story in a two-part series. I started writing the first part during 2009. It was published in July 2013 in a book titled *Ten Seconds*. It was easier for me to write my story in two parts. I am now incorporating the two together to give the reader a "start to finish" journey. It now makes sense to do this. I hope that my story can in some way be a small vision of hope to an individual or a family that has experienced some level of trauma. My goal is to write my story in a way that is easy to read and understand, and that the reader may feel as if he or she is part of the journey. I want readers to find one part which they could relate to and understand the thought process of someone who is desperately trying to recover and heal from a horrific event.

The year was 1990, and it was the beginning of the fall season. Most of the leaves had already started to turn colors, the nights were starting to get cooler, and the days were still hot and humid. Schools were getting ready to begin the new school year, and summer was in its final days. Many families were either on their last vacation of the summer or finishing last-minute school shopping. As for myself, I was a typical young man at the age of twenty-three with not a lot of responsibilities. Life for me consisted of three things: playing baseball, playing softball, and advancing my career. Sundays were designated for our baseball league, and softball took up four of the other six nights.

My weekly work schedule was a typical nine to five, Monday through Friday, plus one night a week. There were times I worked on the road in other districts, which meant being away from home for a week. I would leave after my baseball game on Sunday afternoon and then return home on Saturday evening the following week. My motto was, "When you work, work hard—and when you play, play harder." I have always been a very competitive and goal-oriented person, and this was how I approached almost everything in my life, both personally and with my career. With that said, nothing in this world could have prepared me for what was about to happen to me.

It was something I never saw coming and never imagined happening. It could happen to anyone at any age and at any moment. At the age of twenty-three, it's easy to fall into the misconception that you are invincible from terrible things happening to you, so you don't ever think about any of that. I certainly hadn't, and neither was I prepared for anything like this. I was in for an unimaginable awakening. It took only ten seconds, and those ten seconds changed everything in my life forever—and the lives of those close to me as well.

I was shut down, dead in my tracks, and my life as I knew it was over, as if it had disappeared right in front of me. I was a very lucky and blessed man. As you go on this journey with me, I would like you to think of a couple of questions. Do you have faith? Do you believe there is a God in heaven and that he can perform miracles? Do you believe God has angels who watch over us? My hope in sharing this with you is to help solidify what many may already know and believe, as I do. This is my story!

Chapter 1

Achievements, Accomplishments, and Background

It was September 1, 1990, and our Wisconsin summer was coming to an end. That also meant the baseball and softball seasons were coming to an end as well. Most of us ballplayers looked forward to springtime, when the season got rolling, but on the other hand we sometimes looked forward to the season ending by the time the fall came to pass. Between our baseball league on Sundays and our softball leagues, there were many times we played five nights a week, as well as tournaments on the weekends. Even those of us who loved to play the game that much would become fatigued due to the number of games we played. I had started playing baseball as most young boys had, with T-Ball leagues at the age of five and then little league. High school baseball came next, and I went on to play in the Dairyland League.

The Dairyland League is part of the Wisconsin Baseball Association's amateur men's baseball league. There are approximately sixty teams throughout the state, which are broken up into leagues. Our Dairyland League was made up of eleven to twelve teams in central Wisconsin. I loved the game of baseball and was very fortunate to have excelled at it. I had started playing baseball in the Dairyland League at the age of thirteen. I didn't play on a regular basis due to my age, only when they needed an extra player to fill in. There were others in the area who had played at this early age with other teams as well. Simply being a part of that was very cool, knowing that I could play well enough to have the chance to play when the opportunity was there.

I had started out as a bat boy for the Westboro baseball team when I was eight years old. The following season, when I turned nine, the team had purchased a bat boy uniform for me. It was the same colors as the team's uniforms, and I was the only bat boy at that time with a uniform. Being nine years old with this uniform made me feel more a part of the team. It looked good, and I was so proud of that uniform. I had always showed up for their practices to chase balls in the outfield during batting practice, and I flagged down foul balls. When their practice was over, they always pitched to me so I could take a few swings as well. They always took the time for me to do this. On game days, which were Sunday afternoons, they always made sure that someone from the team picked me up from my home and took me to the game. When the game was over, someone would bring me home at a reasonable time so as to not upset my parents. At nine years old, life was great.

As I grew older, baseball came very natural for me, and it was very easy for me to play at a consistently higher level than most kids my age. Playing in the Dairyland League with one of the surrounding teams was every little leaguer's ultimate goal. I played a lot of softball as well, but baseball always took priority. My positions as a baseball player were pitcher and shortstop, and with softball it was shortstop. In softball, I had played in our Taylor County League for a teamed named the Phonies, because we were sponsored by the Rib Lake Telephone Company. I and some of the other guys from the team also played in the Medford City League as well, with a different team. Medford is the largest city in Taylor County, approximately 4,300 in population.

In 1985, my senior year at Rib Lake High School, our baseball team had made it to the Wisconsin State Baseball Tournament, which was only the second time in our school's history that this had been done. It was a huge achievement for the school, the community, and for us as a team. We came up short of a state championship, but it was an experience that I will forever treasure. What made it more special is that nearly all of us on the team had played together in some form since little league. As an individual achievement, that same year I was selected by the Wisconsin High School Baseball Coaches Association to play in Wisconsin's first High School Baseball All-Star Game. I went in as a pitcher and infielder, and it was an exciting experience. I played on the Wisconsin West Team and was the only player selected from a Class

C school that year. I had a lot going for me during this period of my life, including a full baseball scholarship to Waldorf College, a junior college in Iowa, which I accepted. The school was well-known for its baseball program and a tradition of scholastic and athletic achievements. Coming from a small rural school myself, it seemed to be the perfect fit for me. However, that window of opportunity was closed by somewhat similar but unrelated circumstances. I had cracked a lower vertebrae in by back, near my pelvis, during the summer of 1985. My future had to take a new path.

During this time, I had gone out to California to stay with my older brother and his family. They lived in a city called Chino, which was near Barstow. He had been working road construction out there for several years. I lasted three months before I'd had enough of that, so I came back to Wisconsin. It was within a year or two of that move that I started working in the insurance industry. It was October 1988, and I was twenty years old. This happened by accident, but it was a start of a whole new career for me. I was field recruited by a young, newly promoted district manager in my home area, named Mark Nelson.

The timing of this could not have come at a better time for me. My parents had carried accident insurance on themselves and on all my brothers and me since we were little. Mark was servicing these policies at our home, and this was how I had come in contact with him. Over the next couple of months, he hired me as an in-field sales agent. However, once I was hired, I first had to complete license training school in Minnesota and pass the Wisconsin state insurance exams. Once I had completed that and passed my license exams, I went directly to the company's sales training school the following week, which was also in Minnesota. This training consisted of learning proper product knowledge and gaining the know-how to effectively service our policyholders, both new and existing. I became a claims adjuster to personally assist our policyholders in their homes, to claim any money due to them, and to review their benefits so they understood any other coverages they may have had. Company philosophy and policy was also a major structure throughout this process. These were extremely positive yet difficult classes which I had successfully completed.

After I had successfully gone though these classes and was certified, I needed to be listed with the state of Wisconsin before I could go any further. After this was done, I was ready to enter the field. I would meet Mark every day for morning breakfast meetings. These were designed for brief training and to plan out our daily goals and objectives. We also shared good news throughout the week. As the sales team grew over time, this became more beneficial from a learning standpoint. Mark had set up a seven-week field training program for me, which included the first week as field trainer and trainee week. In addition to this, every Monday night consisted of training meetings that lasted for an hour and a half. These were specifically designed for activity knowledge, product inspection, and team support. The first goal was to be field trained to a PAL Award. PAL stands for "positive action leadership." This is one of the most important awards of company, because it is a trainer and trainee award, and you have only one opportunity at this, which is your very first week out of sales school. Your trainer would show you how to use all of the sales and training tools you learned in sales school. Mark and I achieved this award. There were two levels of PAL Awards: a Gold PAL, which was one hundred new policies in a week, and a Silver PAL, which was sixty polices in one week. Mark and I achieved the Gold PAL.

Next on the agenda was the implementation of what was called the seven-week field training system. Each Monday for the next seven weeks, Mark would field train me to get me off to a fast start and inspect my skills. The rest of the week, I would continue on my own. The seven-week field training is designed to help one focus on the advancement opportunities into management, known as junior executive training (JET). I needed to achieve these necessary requirements in order to advance into the management arena. Mark was a district manager and was in need of a district sales manager. This was where I was headed. These specific steps would begin with what is known as the Initial Award—one hundred new policies written in a two-week period. Then I'd advance to the Pearl Award (100 new policies in a one-week period), and then a Ruby Award (150 new policies written over a two-week period). This would allow me through the various levels of JET (phases I, II, and III) and qualify me for JET IV.

Achieving these took a lot of hard work, dedication, and commitment to the company's philosophy, as well as incentive programs and field training. The willingness to travel and sacrifice the time had to be there as well. All company promotions were based on merit and not seniority. I was single at the time and had nothing holding me back from doing everything possible to achieve this. My baseball scholarship was not part of my future plans, so I needed to place this advancement at the very top of my goal list. I now had to realign my priorities and take full advantage of this opportunity I had at my fingertips. It gave me the ability to take control of my own destiny and success. I was fortunate enough to achieve these steps by September 1989. In November of that same year, I entered and completed the final step, JET IV, at the corporate headquarters in Chicago. There were sixteen other individuals from our six state divisions. The states that made up our division at that time were North Dakota, South Dakota, Iowa, Illinois, Michigan, and Wisconsin.

When these programs were completed, the divisional and national trainers, and the vice president and divisional manager, were to select someone from our class for an award called the MVP award, which stood for "Most Valuable Participant." All of the individuals who were part of the program had reached the same requirements as I had in order to be there, so we were all on the same footing from a production standpoint. The MVP award would be awarded to the one individual who they felt showed the most leadership qualities and knowledge of company philosophy. When it came to the presentation of this award, I was very honored and humbled when the vice president and divisional manger said, "Would Ted Goodrich kindly come up here to accept this award?" I was blown away and somewhat shocked, because this was an award I did not expect to get. I simply wanted to come out of the program knowing more than I did going in, and to learn the know-how to build management skills around my personality in order to be an effective and productive manager. I approached it with the belief that I could not train others or ask them to do something that I myself could not do. Mark Nelson, who had field recruited, hired, and trained me, was a big part of my success. I was now in a position to do for others what was done for me. All things considered, I had a taste of success on both fronts. I was very proud of these achievements and what I had done to this point, as were my parents and my three brothers. I was now a full-fledged district sales manager, running my own sales team and reporting directly to Mark. Things were starting to turn around for me.

With that said, our baseball season was now over, and the last softball tournament of the year was at hand. This tournament was in a small town called Prentice. It is located approximately twenty minutes north from my hometown of Westboro. Each year the Prentice community holds an event called the Prentice Progress Days. We have several communities in the surrounding area that hold similar events to promote their town and what it has to offer regarding attractions and the like. These little events can bring in a lot of outside people to visit our smaller rural communities. The events are held at different times of the summer in order to maximize the exposure for each town. When I say outside people, I am referring to those within the counties around us, along with the vacationers and visitors to our area. Each community has its own unique attractions and outdoor activities that make them great vacations destinations. For example, a small community a few minutes north of where I lived is a small town called Ogema. One would not know that Ogema is the home to Timm's Hill, the highest point in the state of Wisconsin. Rib Mountain in Central Wisconsin's Wausau is first thought of, in part, due to the flat landscape and the ski hill on Rib Mountain. Timm's Hill in Ogema has so much more to offer, such as beautiful sightseeing, hiking trails, nearby camping, and fishing. My hometown has an event called Westboro Country Days, and the town I now live in has one called Rib Lake Ice Age Days. The corridor to the Wisconsin north woods begins here in these rural areas.

Chapter 2

The Day That Changed My Life Forever

Labor Day weekend is the last holiday prior to the school year beginning, and playing in this softball tournament was an annual gig for us. This year was no different. We registered with our usual team, as we had done so many times before. The day for me started out as any other weekend when we had a ball tournament scheduled.

The date was September 1, 1990. We had a midmorning Saturday game scheduled, which meant getting to the park about a half hour earlier to do pregame warm ups such as stretching, throwing, and some hitting practice. Every team has this available to them if they arrived to the park early enough, and if time permitted before the start of each game throughout the tournament. This usually took about twenty to thirty minutes. We had a 10:00 a.m. game scheduled, the temperature was extremely warm for this time of the day, and the humidity was already high enough to make it uncomfortable to play.

A little informational note here: much of the events and the descriptions I am going to be describing about this day as it unfolded have been told to me and explained to me over time by my teammates, family, close friends, and the physicians whose care I was under. It is not uncommon for someone to not remember details leading up to or after something like my accident occurs. These details have been researched and verified by those who were there through interviews or documentation, medical records, and my own personal knowledge.

Between our scheduled games and depending on whether we won or lost, we would usually hang around for a while and watch a few of the games that followed, because we may be playing one of those teams later on in the tournament. However, on this particular weekend we didn't do that at all. We wanted to find someplace to go where it was cooler, because it was so hot and humid. As the day went on, the playing conditions made it seem as though we were playing in an oven. Between our games, we would go where there was air-conditioning to cool down and rest up for upcoming games.

Staying hydrated was also a big factor. We had decided to go to the Prentice Golf Club House to play cards, get a little something to eat, and have a few drinks. Our next scheduled game was midday, and we ended up playing one more in the afternoon because we had lost our second game. While playing during these times during the day, the humidity was nearly unbearable, and temperatures had reached 95 degrees. Needless to say, we were pretty exhausted by the time we had finished our last game of the day. When that last game was over, we had no desire to be outside anymore. We gathered our equipment and got the heck out of there. We headed to one of the taverns in town. All that we had on our minds was air-conditioning, a few cold drinks, and getting something to eat. We stayed at the bar for an hour or two playing cards, throwing darts, and shooting some pool while making plans to head back to Rib Lake for a street dance that was going on later in the evening. There was a nationally known band playing in town that night, and one of the band members was a native of Rib Lake. The band had a top hit on the charts at the time, and most of the guys wanted to see him play. Some of the team had gone to school with the guy, and I knew him as well because he had given me guitar lessons when I was younger; I also graduated with his youngest brother.

The plan was to hang out together at the street dance, watch the band play, and then finish the softball tournament the next day. Some of us were going to go home, shower, and change clothes before meeting up at the dance. A few people were going straight to the dance. One of my teammates and I left at the same time. He was parked ahead of me, so I said that I would follow him back. I was going to stop at home and change clothes, and I thought that he was going to change at my place as well. When we passed through Westboro by my apartment, he continued on to Rib Lake. I assumed his change of clothes was at one of the other guy's places, or he was simply going to the dance in his baseball clothes. I turned into my driveway as he continued on to Rib Lake, which was about ten minutes from my apartment.

About an hour and a half passed, and most of the guys had already met up at the dance and were wondering where I was. My buddy who was driving in front of me told them that I was behind him and had turned into my apartment. They thought that I was probably still at home getting ready, taking a rest, or I'd been sidetracked with a couple of other buddies at the dance. At the time I was renting a second-story apartment, and I had been there for nearly a year and a half. My younger brother Randy and his wife were living across the street from me a little to the south. The next closest building structure to my place was a church, also just to the south and seventy-five feet away. My other neighbors lived just past this church; their home was maybe two hundred feet from my apartment. He and his wife were both school teachers, and I knew them well because I'd had both of them at one point during high school. They were having a Labor Day cookout with friends and some of the other teachers from school. My neighbors and other people there later said that they had seen me turn into my driveway at about six o'clock that evening. My apartment staircase was somewhat visible from the main road, but not the bottom at ground level due to shrubs and small trees. Many cars had passed and had not noticed a thing—and why should they?

The guys I was going to meet up with were still wondering where I was, and they said they had tried calling me. With the line of work I was in, it was always important to be punctual, so it was not like me to not show up or be late for things. My friend Gary Hohl, who was our team's pitcher, said that he was waiting for me at the Little Bohemia the whole time, and he had called my apartment about five times. The Little Bohemia is a bowling alley that he and his family have owned for many years in Rib Lake. This was our central meeting spot in town when we had team-related things going on, or if we were getting together. He said he never gave it a second thought of anything serious happening, only that it seemed odd that I had not yet shown up.

Chapter 3

Being Found:
Was It by Chance, or Was It Fate?

It was now approaching eight thirty in the evening. A couple from the cookout decided to leave and head back to Rib Lake, where they lived. The couple was my high school baseball coach and his wife, Dick and Teri Iverson. We were close friends and knew each other very well. When they left, they needed to turn around to go home. They had several options to choose from in order to turn their vehicle around. One option was to do a quick U-turn and head back. Another option was to turn around in the church parking lot between the church and where they were parked. The third option for them was to turn around in my brother's driveway, which was somewhat kitty-corner from my apartment and a little bit closer to where they were originally parked. I truly believe that it was only by the grace of God that they decided to turn around in my driveway, and that was extremely fortunate for me. They originally didn't intend to stop in and visit, but they said that they saw a light shinning from inside my car. They didn't think anything of it but decided to stop in to say hi and tell me about the light. They both got out of their vehicle and walked around the corner of the house on the west side. They saw me lying on the ground at the bottom of my staircase. I was laying partly on the grass and on the sidewalk. They believed at first that maybe I had laid down to rest and had fallen asleep, or maybe I'd even passed out. They would have no reason to think otherwise. They called out to me as they walked closer.

Still not knowing anything was wrong, they called out to me again as they approached where I was.

When they got next to me, they knew something was definitely wrong. I had some bleeding from my ears and my nose. They tried to wake me but were unable to do so; I was unconscious and unresponsive. Teri yelled for Dick to go up to my apartment and call 911. He ran up the stairs, and when he got to the top of my staircase to go inside, he yelled down that it was locked and couldn't get in. My land lady had passed away nearly two months earlier, so there was no one in her lower level part of the home, and of course those doors were locked as well. Dick ran over to my brother's home across the street; they knew my brother and his wife as well. Randy and his wife were out on their front deck when he came running across the street yelling, "Teddy is hurt, and we need to call 911." Dick explained what was wrong, and Randy immediately called 911. Randy also thought it best to call my parents right away. My parents lived west of town about three miles out. After hearing what my brother had explained, my mom and dad wanted to get my youngest brother Rodney and have him ride up as well. He was visiting a neighbor, so it took a few extra minutes to contact him and pick him up.

While Dick was doing this, Teri stayed with me; talking to me and trying to get some response from me, but she was not able to do so. Within fifteen minutes, the Rib Lake first responders had arrived, and the ambulance was minutes behind them.

My parents and Rodney arrived shortly after the first responders. By this time it was nearly three hours from the estimated time I'd fallen down my stairs. Living in a small community, it did not very take very long for word to spread on what had happened. A few in town came to see if they could help.

The police were now arriving on the scene as well. My parents said that they were scared when they arrived at my apartment. They did not fully know what had happened, and getting information was difficult with all the commotion. One of the EMTs, whose name was Tammy Graumann, approached them at one point and briefly explained what they knew of my condition so far. Tammy told my mom and dad that it appeared I had fallen down the stairs and hit my head on the sidewalk. I had what initially appeared to be a skull fracture on the right side of my head above the ear. She also explained that because there was no real amount of blood loss, this indicated that I had possibly suffered a closed head injury. Tammy explained if this were the case, my brain was most likely swelling, and that any potential bleeding was going in and around my brain. She said although I was unresponsive, I was still alive, and they were very close to having me ready for transport. It would be best for my parents to head for the hospital. My mom said that Tammy told them to drive carefully; rushing wasn't going to do them or Teddy any good, if they drove too fast and got into an accident themselves.

My parents and Rodney got in the car and started out, as they were asked to do. The ambulance started out about ten minutes later and even passed them about three-quarters of the way to the hospital. My mom said my dad was driving, and when he pulled over as the ambulance passed them, she had the most terrified feeling that she had ever had. She also said that none of them said much along the way; they had a feeling of numbness and shock.

The first medical facility which I was taken to was our county hospital, which at the time was known as Taylor County Hospital. It has since been renamed to Medford Memorial Health Center, and it was approximately twenty-five miles south of my apartment. We have a local newspaper in our area called *The Star News*. The following was written and sent in to the newspaper by longtime friends and neighbors John and Geraldine Poncek. Their article was positioned in the Vox Pop section of the newspaper. This was posted a week after my accident, but I wanted to place it here because they wanted to give appreciation to the Iversons for taking the time to stop by my apartment that day.

> Westboro man alive thanks to the Iversons of Rib Lake. We would like to praise Dick and Teri Iverson of Rib Lake for their alertness and thoughtfulness that saved the life of Teddy Goodrich of Westboro last Saturday evening, Sept. 1. About 8 p.m., the Iversons left some friend's house and had to turn their car around in Teddy's driveway when they noticed that the dome light was on in his car. They decided to stop and tell him about it. When they got to the outside staircase of Teddy's apartment, they found him lying at the bottom of the steps unconscious. It was later discovered that Teddy was seen arriving home at 6pm, so he had already been lying there two hours. The doctors reported that it was very fortunate that Teddy was found when he was because time was of the essence in his condition.

He had received a severe blow to the head from the fall down the steps that required emergency surgery at the Marshfield hospital. At last report from his family, Teddy is doing very well and should be returning home soon. Had it not been for the Iversons' thoughtfulness and taking the extra time to tell Teddy about the light, it may well have been too late. He may not have been discovered until Monday morning. Our special Thanks to Dick and Teri for saving our friend's life.

I'm sure we speak for many of Teddy's friends.

John and Geraldine Poncek, Westboro

Chapter 4

Was It Really the Dome Light?

My brother Randy and his wife had stayed back at my apartment until things settled down and the scene cleared out a bit. Initial indications from the police were that while at the top of my staircase, my softball spikes got tangled up or caught on my door mat going into my apartment. For some reason I hadn't changed into my tennis shoes at the ball field when we finished playing our last game of the day. My spikes getting tangled up in my door mat caused me to lose my balance, and I fell backward down the staircase and hit my head on the sidewalk at the bottom; this would explain the skull fracture that I had. It looked as though it happened quickly, because my house key was bent and broken off in the door lock. It was about twenty-five steps that I had fallen down. I had no other broken bones, scratches, or anything other than the apparent skull fracture.

My brother and sister-in-law were getting ready to leave and head for the hospital. Before they left, Randy wanted to make sure my car was locked up that the dome light was off so that my car battery would not run dead overnight. When Randy went to close the driver's side door, he said that it was already closed. He then went around to close the passenger door, on the chance I had walked around to open it for some reason and had left it ajar. When he checked that door; he said that it was closed as well. He checked the back hatch and then the dome light switch, the head light switch, and the overhead reading lamp switches. None of them were on at all—not a single one. Randy said he thought to himself, *That can't be right.* He said that he double-checked to be sure of this. He had a blank look on his face and thought, *How is the dome light on?* He said that the hairs on his arms stood up, and he got goose bumps. Then the next thing he thought of was, *How could Dick and Teri have seen the dome light on?* It didn't make any sense. This was the second thing that seemed to me to be by the grace of God. There are several instances throughout my story that are similar to this. Before leaving, he told the Rib Lake police chief the car was locked up, and he explained to him what he'd found out about the car. The chief was at a loss of words as well. Randy and his wife then left for the Medford hospital.

They said that they talked about it on the way, and then again later when they were driving to St. Joseph's Hospital Trauma Center at Marshfield. Some of the things they talked about were how was Ted's dome light was on? Not only how or why was it on, but what was on? Besides that, how was it bright enough to be seen from the roadway at the end of my driveway, where my friends had turned around? The car that I had at the time was a 1987 Chevrolet Iroc style Camaro. This was a low-profile car, and my friends had a four-wheel-drive Ford Bronco II. The Ford Bronco II would be higher off the ground and above equal eye level of my car. The sun was setting in the west, and on top of that, my car was parked seventy to eighty feet from the main road. From an electrical perspective, there was no mechanical reason that my dome light should have been on. Yet this was what my coach and his wife said they saw when turning around in my driveway. They said that they saw a light shining in my car, and that led them to stop. Naturally, one would assume it was the dome light. To actually see the dome light itself in my car, you practically need to be standing next to the door, bending over and looking up through the passenger or driver windows. So how could the light have been on and be bright enough for them to see it as they did? To this day, I often think of this, and I am still convinced there was a reason my friends Dick and Teri passed on three alternative ways in which they could have turned their vehicle around. I believe they were meant to find me and were guided to turn into my driveway. It was fate, and was meant to work out that way!

Chapter 5

Initial Medical Confirmation

My parents and my brother Rodney had arrived at the hospital not too long after the ambulance. When they arrived, they went straight to the emergency room, where someone was waiting for them. They said that the emergency room physician on call was tending to me now and that he was not able to come out and see them right away; someone would be out soon with more information. Eventually one of the nurses came out and talked to my family, assuring them that I was receiving the best possible medical attention and that the doctor would be out as soon as he could with more information about my condition. When he did come out to see them, he confirmed that I had suffered what is called a traumatic brain injury, also known as TBI. He also explained that a severe, closed-head injury of this nature was a trauma they were not able to accommodate, and they were preparing to transport me to Marshfield

St. Joseph's Hospital Trauma Center was thirty-six miles south, or about a forty-five-minute drive. When my parents asked of my condition, the doctor explained to them that due to the time I had been lying there, I had major brain swelling and was bleeding on and around the brain, so much that not much brain activity was observed through his examination. The only thing they could do was provide me with specific medication to keep the my brain from swelling more than it had, and to stabilize me for the transport to Marshfield. My parents asked if they could see me, and the doctor said they could for a little bit while the staff prepared me for transport.

When they came in to see me, they broke down crying. My mom said that she walked over to me, gave me a hug and a kiss on my forehead, and said to me that it was going to be okay, that they were here for me and loved me. When the medical staff was removing some clothing, they needed to roll me on my side a little bit, and my mom was still holding me near my head. As they rolled me over onto my side, blood started to come out of my mouth. She said that it was like I had started choking on my own blood. Then all of a sudden I gagged and spat out a mouthful of blood all over her. She screamed out because it scared her so much, and it had happened so quickly. But she didn't let go of my head where she was holding me. She said that she had my blood in her hair, on her face, and on her clothes. Whenever I now think back of this happening to her, I can't begin to imagine what she was going through as a parent. I cannot find words to describe the emotions, feelings, and thoughts that my mom and dad were having to deal with, or how Rodney was coping with this. One minute they were at home doing their usual things, and the next minute they received a call that their son was injured and an ambulance was called. They said they never once imagined that things would unfold as they had. My parents were again asked to head out ahead of the ambulance, and to drive carefully. My mom had cleaned up a bit, and they began the drive to St. Joseph's in Marshfield.

By this time, news of this had reached some of my friends and teammates at the dance. The news they'd heard was that I had died, that I'd fallen down my stairs and died when I'd hit my head on the sidewalk at the bottom of the stairs. At first it was thought to be some sort of misunderstanding—until they heard it from more sources. A couple of them immediately drove down to the Marshfield Trauma Center upon hearing the news from several sources. Two of them were my best friend Scott Zondlo and his wife, Renee. Scott and I had known each other since kindergarten. We played ball together and did nearly everything with one another. When in high school, by chance we each had Ford Pinto hatchbacks as our first cars. His was yellow and mine was red. They were identical other than the color. Our buddies started calling us the Pinto Brothers. It was something we still pimped each other about once in a while. We were all in the same grade and graduated together.

Scott had said when he and Renee had heard of the news, it was about midnight. He and Renee couldn't believe it and had to drive down to find out for themselves. When they arrived, they met my family while they were still in the waiting area. Scott had asked if it was true what he and Renee had heard: that I had died. They told them what had happened and updated them on everything, adding that I was now in surgery. They were like family to me and my parents, so they waited all night with them till my surgery was over, and they heard the news with the rest of my family: I had made it through the surgery. My mom and dad were the first to come in and see me when they got the okay. My parents later vouched for Scott and Renee, and they were able to come in and see me for a little bit with the rest of my family. Scott said that he and Renee were shocked and very scared for me. One of the things that Scott said to me while grabbing my big toe was to say, "Teddy, you are going to be all right. You are going to pull through this, big guy." He said when he did that, the peepers and buzzers flared up, and a nurse came rushing in to check on me, which scared them a little bit. Scott and Renee stayed for a little while and then went back home.

Another good friend of mine, Dan Fliehs, drove down after hearing the news. I was still in surgery when he got there. The staff there would only say to him that they could release information only to immediate family members at this time. Dan said, "That's okay, I understand that. I just want to know if Teddy is alive and going to be okay." My family didn't know that Dan was there; they were in another part of the unit at that time. Dan understood that the nurses couldn't tell him anything, but it frustrated him to no end. He said that all he wanted to know was whether or not I was alive, but the nurse couldn't release any information to him. He didn't know where my parents were at the time, so he ended up driving back to Rib Lake with no information and waited to hear of any news.

The softball team ended up forfeiting our games for the rest of the tournament and did not play on Sunday. No one was up to playing at all after this had happened. They did not find out till the next day that I was still alive and had made it through the surgery. The surgery itself took a total of fourteen hours, and only time was going to spell out how things were going to look from that point on. From what I understand, many prayers went out for me and my family that night. Their prayers did not go unanswered.

Chapter 6

From Bad to Worse

When my mom and dad initially arrived at the Marshfield Hospital, they were met by a nurse who waiting for them. She explained that Medford Memorial personnel had called and notified them that I was coming in, so they were prepared with the specifics of my trauma and were tending to me now and running tests. After some time, the doctor came out and explained to my parents about my condition, adding that unfortunately things didn't look very well. He confirmed that I indeed had a fractured skull above my ear on the right side of my head. He also explained that with this kind of traumatic brain injury, especially with a severe closed-head injury, time was of the essence. Because of the time I had laid there, my brain had swelled so much, and there was significant bleeding and clotting within and around my brain, which formed two large masses.

The first blood mass was located near the front of my head, which is the right and left frontal lobe area, and the other was on the right temporal lobe just above my right ear, toward the side. It was also explained to my family that they had to medicinally induce me into a deep coma, to keep my brain from further swelling. My mom and dad asked if they could see me, but they were not able to just yet. While waiting, they were thanking the ambulance personnel.

Tammy Graumann was one of the Rib Lake EMT first responders who rode down in the ambulance with me that night. She knew my family very well and was also a friend of mine. She said to my mom and dad that it was a long, rough ride for Teddy from Medford. Mom asked, "How do you mean?" Tammy said that they had lost me four times. My mom said that she didn't understand what Tammy was saying to her. Tammy explained that I had died four separate times, but they were able to revive me by jump-starting my heart with a defibrillator. She also said that she was sorry they were having to go through this, and she hoped things would turn out for the best. They should stay strong and have faith. The night had been so overwhelming for everyone, and my mom was in a form of shock and still didn't fully grasp what was said to her. She repeated, "He died four times on the way here from Medford?" Tammy had said yes, but they were able to somehow revive me each time, and I was a real fighter. My mom said she didn't even know what to say, and she and Dad looked at each other. After hearing of this later, I do not believe it to always be true when it is said that the patient is the one in the most pain. Parents and family members are often in as much or more pain at seeing a loved one go through something like this, because they feel so helpless and there is absolutely nothing they can do. Everything was out of their control, and sometimes that is what is most scary.

My brothers and sister-in-law were now in the waiting area with my parents. They told them what the ambulance personnel had said, and the doctors were running more tests and examining me now. The doctor later came out to explain my condition and what decisions needed to be made, or at least what the immediate options were. It was explained that I was on life support but was stabilized as best I could be under the circumstances. Also, tests indicated that clinically there was minimal to no brain activity. The amount of brain swelling and the bleeding in and around my brain was extensive. This was primarily due to the extent of my fall and the amount of time I had laid there. My family asked if I was in a lot of pain. The doctor said that I was not in any pain. My mom and dad came in to see me first. The doctor said not to be alarmed by how I look, and they should know that I was in no pain. My brothers came in shortly after with the understanding that it could possibly be to say their last good-byes. My oldest brother, Conrad, was on his way to the hospital; he worked on road construction and had been out of town. It was hard to reach him initially, and I later learned that making the decision of removing me from life support before he arrived was not an option at this point. My mom and dad wanted the entire family to be part of any decision that needed to be made, and they wanted to make sure everyone had a chance to say good-bye if that were the case. The decision to go with the surgery was still an option for them. It was risky, but it was the best option if one compared it to the first alternative.

I would like to make special mention here in honor of the memory of Tammy Graumann. Tammy had since lost her long battle to cancer and is dearly missed by her husband, family, and friends. I owe her and the Rib Lake first responders so much for their quick judgment and treatment for me while I was under their care that evening.

Chapter 7

The Night God Took My Hand

This is where I believed I woke from my coma. I believed that I was awake during this period of time as my parents were by my bedside, and the doctor was explaining to them the possible treatment options and the possible outcomes for me from this. I could hear the doctor say that the likelihood of me coming out of this without major brain damage was unlikely, or I could stay in a coma indefinitely. From the medical side of things, there was too much damage to the brain and too much swelling, and too much time had passed, causing the blood masses. He said to them that I was alive as the result of life support. They also discussed surgery and the possible outcomes of that.

As they were talking, I was listening to them, but their voices were faint and soft. I had mumbled to them to speak a little louder because I could not hear them very well. They didn't seem to hear me or acknowledge me. Most of their eye contact seemed to be on the doctor and what he was saying to them. I was aware of the tube going into my mouth and down my throat, and my mouth was taped. I also knew that there were hoses going up into my nose, and that could be why I couldn't talk loud or clear enough for them to hear me. I again asked them to speak a little louder so I could better hear what they were saying. They continued to talk as though they weren't listening to me. Once again I asked them to speak louder, and I asked why they were not listening to me. It was as though they were talking about me like I was not there. As their conversation went on, I seemed to become more alert, and I heard them talking about the options available, which was to perform surgery to release pressure off the brain and remove the blood mass—or a more final option, which was to remove me from life support and let me pass away peacefully.

It was at that point it hit me that they could not hear me at all. I started to try to get their attention in some way. I tried harder to talk louder in a way that they could hear me. There was only so much I felt I could do, but they still wouldn't acknowledge me in any way. I started to talk louder and louder. It got to the point to where I was screaming up to them. It was a terrifying feeling, and I didn't understand what was going on. It was as though I was looking at them through my eyes and my chest, and like there was a thick glass barrier between us. It seemed so bizarre. As I listened to them, I could hear them discussing the alternatives, and I panicked. I was scared and started to cry. I began to scream up to them, "Why can't any of you hear me? I am right here. I'm alive, and I can hear you!. Please, just one of you look down at me. I am here! Somebody, please help me and do something!" I began pounding upward on the inside of my chest to get their attention, and then I started kicking and pounding. The easiest way to describe it is to compare this to lying on the floor on your stomach, and you begin pounding your fists and then kicking your feet on the floor, just as a child throws a temper tantrum. As I explained earlier, it was like there was this thick glass like barrier between us.

This seemed to go on for a long time. I was still crying, asking them, "Why are you guys not hearing me? I am alive here. Please don't let me die! Just look down at me and see for yourselves!" Nothing I was trying to do seemed to get their attention. After some time passed, I realized they were not going to hear me—and because of that, I was possibly going to die. My mom and dad were going to let me die here and not try to help me. This was what was going through my mind. Whether or not it was what they were thinking, I didn't know. I can't imagine them thinking that at all, but I couldn't understand what was happening. My mom was crying, and I could see it was difficult for her and Dad to discuss things with the doctor. I was still yelling loud to get their attention, but not as I was before. I was crying and sobbing, asking them, "Why would you do this to me and let this happen?" Then as time passed, all I could hear was low mumbling, and I couldn't make out what they were saying anymore. I kept muttering, "Please don't let me die," over and over again. I was crying and was scared that no one was going to hear me or help me.

It seemed like hours had passed. It almost felt as though I was going to be buried alive. I grew very tired and started to realize what was about to maybe happen, and I didn't like what I was thinking. I was so exhausted and tired; I could not yell anymore, could not lift my hands, and wasn't able to move my legs. It was like my body went limp. I had no more strength left, and I found myself lying there and staring straight up to the ceiling. All of my strength was gone. I would occasionally move my eyes to see what was going on. I felt like I was in a stare-down with myself, and I was afraid to blink or close my eyes for fear that I may not open them again.

While I was thinking of all this, things suddenly began to feel weird. I didn't know exactly what it was, only that things seemed a little odd and different. I began to feel this warm sensation run through my body. It felt as though a very warm flow of water covered me, but I knew I was not wet. Soon after, I started to feel a sudden sense of calm, and a relaxed sensation come over me. I did not have the frantic or scared feeling anymore. Within what seemed to be minutes of having this warm feeling, I felt the warm touch of someone taking my right hand. It was a very soft and soothing touch. I immediately teared up and thought, *Finally someone has come into the room and realized I am awake. Things are finally going to be okay.* I was still in my little stare-down with the ceiling. I turned my eyes and my head to see who this person was, but no one was there.

Everything got really quiet, and I froze. I don't remember a single thought going through my head at this moment. Then within the blink of an eye, I was looking at my parents and the doctor standing near me at my bedside, talking. I could not hear them or make out what they were saying; I was able to see their mouths moving, but there was no sound. I found myself not concentrating on them anymore and wondering what was going on with me. What was happening, how was I here, and how they were there? I was standing in the far corner of the room, looking down on them and watching them. I looked to see if I was standing on anything, and I wasn't—yet I was near the ceiling and by myself. How? I wasn't afraid of falling, and neither was I trying to balance myself. I was simply standing there with my head a few inches from the ceiling, staring at myself in my bed, my mom and dad, and the doctor. I wasn't scared anymore and felt at peace. I still felt this warm, soft touch of someone holding my hand and comforting me.

When I looked down at my body, my parents, and the doctor, the room seemed very normal—if one could really call it normal. I decided to turn my head, look to my right, and see how I felt this warm touch on my right hand. When I did this, I looked down at my hand and then moved my eyes upward to see how this was happening. I was somewhat startled by what I saw. It was nothing but white light, soft and glowing. I looked around, and it wasn't a light shining anywhere from that part of the room, because I was in the corner and walls were next to me. It also was not a light shining in from another room, and there was no light on my left side. The room was lightly lit from the normal room lights, but nothing would explain this white light right next to me. I still felt someone holding my hand, and I started thinking, *I can't be here alone. I just can't be.* I started to look back and forth, over and over again. I never said a word, and after some time passed, the light I was seeing slowly grew brighter and brighter. In a few moments it became so bright that I couldn't see anything at all. It never hurt my eyes, and I didn't even have to squint or anything. Everything was so quiet and peaceful, and when I thought the light couldn't get any brighter, it did. But never once did it hurt my eyes.

At this point, I thought that I knew what was happening, and I kept looking left to right. I still couldn't see anything, and I wasn't saying anything at this point. The entire room became like a bright whiteout. If what was happening to me now was what I thought was happening ... I didn't want it to happen. I now found myself saying, "If this is what I think it is, please don't take me. I really wanna stay. Please let me stay. I only want them to know I'm here and let me wake up." After a few more minutes, the light got so bright that I put my left hand up above my eyes as if the sun was shining directly in them, though my eyes still did not hurt; I simply wanted to see into the light. I was looking for someone to explain this or help me understand what was happening. Then I felt the soothing hold on my hand start to slip away, and the light slowly faded. It was like a dimmer switch in a home, and the light went dimmer and dimmer. I said, "No, please don't go. Don't leave me here alone. Just stay with me. I need you to stay and watch over me. I want to let them know I am here, and I want to wake up!" I became frightened of what might happen to me. I thought to myself, *Ted, what did you just do?*

At that point, everything went dark. The next thing that I remember, I was lying in my bed and looking up at the ceiling again. This time there was a small group of people I didn't know looking down at me. The first thing I thought of was, *Here we go again.* But this time it was different. They actually acknowledged me. I heard someone say to me, "Welcome back, Ted. How do you feel?" Then he asked me if I could understand them. These were doctors and nurses. I didn't know who said this to me, but they knew that I was awake!

However, prior to my waking up and seeing these people in front of me, my friend Mark Nelson was there when I first opened my eyes and said my first words. As odd as this may sound, Mark said that he was talking to me as he always had when he came down to see me, and he was looking out the window. He said all of a sudden he heard this soft voice say, "Hey, you are my big fat DM" (district manager), and all of a sudden he said a bunch of beepers and buzzers went off. The next thing he knew, people were rushing into the room and rushing him out, saying that he needed to leave, and they escorted him to another room. He didn't know what was going on, or what he'd done. I had just awakened from my coma of about ten days.

Chapter 8

A Decision to Make: A Parent's Worst Nightmare

Throughout life, parents have to make many decisions on behalf of their children, from the day their kids are born through the time they leave the home. Even after that, parents are always parents, and the kids are always their children. Being a parent isn't the easiest job in the world, and much of the time it does seem like a full-time job. There are always little crises that need to be addressed. "My best friend is mad at me and won't talk to me," or "So and so sat by my best friend at the lunch table." Even when you are grown and no longer living with their parents, they always seem to have advice to share with you, whether or not you want to hear it. As a rule of thumb, children are expected to outlive their parents. Unfortunately, this is not always the case. What must go through a parent's mind when faced with a life-or-death decision when it involves a child, regardless of age?

Knowing the uncertainty or unimaginable life ahead of him if he survives such a tragedy, or having guilt if the parent chooses to let him die peacefully, because the odds are so against him and everything medically suggests it may be for the best. As the saying sometimes goes, "Heads, I win; tails, you lose."

I am now the father of two beautiful children, two little girls whom I love and cherish with all my being; you will come to know them at a later point. It would kill me and tear at my heart if I were in a situation like my parents were forced to be in with me. I was single at the time, and this decision was talked over with my entire family, but the burden came down to one person: my mom. Either way, it would be a decision she would have to live with for the rest of her life, and it could possibly affect the lives of the rest of the family. The reason the decision was ultimately my mom's was because my biological father had died when I was thirteen years old. My mom had later remarried. From a legal perspective, my mom had the final call. I don't wish to infer anything other than that point, as my stepfather has been my brothers' and my dad for years, and he was just as much affected by this as any good dad would be. The doctors explained all of the options available to them and what the possible consequences could be for each one. There were no guarantees and no crystal ball for them to look into. They had only their hearts to guide them. They chose the surgery. To them, there was never really any doubt and nothing to think about. However, they still needed to go through the process of knowing all the available options. Even though it wasn't a quick decision, taking me off life support was not an option for them.

To perform this surgery, the doctors had to do a craniotomy and remove part of my skull to let the brain swelling have a way to expand, so they could suction out as much of the blood mass as they could. The surgery was not a cure—it was risky, and the chance of my dying during the surgery was still a strong possibility ... but it was hope, a chance that I wouldn't have had if they had removed me from life support. The following is the operative report from the Marshfield Clinic and Hospital Trauma Center. It describes the efforts and delicacy of the kind of surgery they had to perform.

>Theodore W. Goodrich
>9-2-90
>Dr. XXXXX, MD, Neurosurgeon
>DR. XXXXX, PAC, Assistant
>XXXXXX, CRNA and XXXXXX, MD, Anesthesia

>Preop Diagnosis: Right temporoparietal acute epidural hematoma

>Postop Diagnosis: Same

>Operation: Right temporoparietal craniotomy, evacuation of acute epidural hematoma and control of bleeding, insertion of epidural

drains. After the patient was initially intubated in the emergency room for airway protection and to allow him to be sedated for the CT scan, because of his agitation, he was taken to the CT room where a CT scan of the head revealed a large acute epidural hematoma with significant mass effect. Arrangements were made for the prompt surgery and a preoperative evaluation completed quickly. The proposed surgery, including its indications, risks and alternates, was discussed with the patients' mother and other family members. They were in agreement with the plan to proceed directly to surgery and, therefore, the patient was taken to the operating room. In the operating room, general endotracheal anesthesia was induced, the head was shaved and the appropriate intravenous and monitoring lines established.

Then the patient was positioned supine with the head turned towards the left side and supported in the Mayfield horseshoe head rest in the usual fashion for a right temporoparietal craniotomy. After the head had been prepped, the proposed incision was marked out as a curvilinear incision extending vertically in front o the right ear, overlying the area of the clot as demonstrated on the CT scan. After the head was draped, the incision was made and carried down to the temporalis fascia and the skull. Raney clips and bipolar cautery were used for scalp hemostasis.

The temporal muscle was divided with the cutting cauter. The temporalis was then reflected and the skin edges retracted with self-retaining retractors. The fracture line, which had been demonstrated on the scout film of the CT, was noted in the exposure. A bur hole was placed in the lower temporal region at the edge of the fracture line. Then the Midas-Res craniotome was used to remove a bone flap from in front of the fracture line. The clot was noted through the bur hold and the craniectomy. It was noted that the clot was variable in consistency with some areas quite adherent to the dura and other areas relatively softer and able to be suctioned. It was necessary to remove some bone from the area posterior to the fracture line also in order to get adequate exposure. The epidural had dissected the dura up from the floor of the middle fossa in its posterior region as demonstrated on the X-ray and also had dissected far posteriorly and superiorly. Using the suction, clot was removed from all of these areas until the dura was exposed. The superior and posterior margins of the clot were not treated as aggressively leaving a bit of adherent clot because of the danger of bleeding in an inaccessible area.

This clot will liquify and come out the craniectomy in time and certainly was not large enough in volume to produce any significant mass affect. The brain itself was relatively slack and did not readily expand at surgery, although this may also be due to the preoperative Mannitol which he received just prior to surgery. After all of the significant clot had been removed and hemostasis secured in the dura, including a few more vigorous bleeders which were cauterized carefully, the wound was again thoroughly irrigated. The Jackson-Pratt drains were brought out through separate stab incisions and were left in the epidural plane. Hemostasis was secured in the temporalis muscle, which was then reapproximated with O vicryl in a running suture. Thrombin was used for hemostasis in the epidural space and a few small pledgets of Surgicel also. With the temporalis muscle closed over the drains, hemostasis was secured superficially in the wound and then the wound was closed with a single layer closure of 3-0 Nurolon. The drains were sutured in place to the skin and then dressings were placed on the wound. The patient was taken to the recovery room, still intubated, with the plan initially to leave him intubated overnight with sedation if necessary to better control his agitation and also allow a follow-up CT scan in the morning. After the CT, if everything looked satisfactory, we may allow his medications to wear off and, if he appears to be recovering well, wean him off the ventilator. Blood loss was estimated at less than 300 mL, during the procedure and counts were correct at the end of the procedure. No blood was given during surgery. The patient tolerated the procedure well throughout and was taken to the recovery room in stable condition. His pupils were equal in the recovery room. His vital signs remained stable in the recovery room. He will subsequently be taken to intensive care for postoperative observations.

The surgery took about fourteen total hours, plus recovery room time. It was a risky and delicate surgery, but none of the options were favorable to a positive outcome. My family said that they would accept me in any way, if I were survive this. My brothers told me that Mom would say, "This is what families do. We pull together no matter what. Do what is right, even if there was only the slightest chance of hope. That is the way to go."

If they hadn't made that decision, I certainly wouldn't be here today, and it goes to show that people can come out of comas and recover. To this day, my physicians are still amazed at the unbelievable recovery I have made. There is no medical explanation of my recovery; it normally doesn't ever happen this way, not when it comes to injuries to the brain, especially the one I had endured. My parents and family made the right call by approving the surgery. The neurosurgeon met with them to explain how the surgery went, saying that I held up remarkably well and made it through this critical stage, but they wouldn't know anything more till I woke up and they could run further tests. He went on to explain that the neuropsychologists would later see what extent of damage was done, once they started to work with me, but that was only if I was to come out of my coma. Things were far from being out of the woods. He also said that they could not remove me from life support yet because I was unable to breathe on my own. He said that my arms would still be tied down to the bed at the wrists, to keep me from pulling out the tubes or IVs. He said patients are known to pull these out when agitated or confused. In my case, if I were to wake up and was disoriented, I could start pulling at them, which would not be a good thing. It was a safety precaution for me so that I would not have this happen.

After some time, I did indeed come out of my coma, and they began some basic tests. I was eventually taken off life support because I began to breathe on my own, and my heart was stable. I wasn't able to communicate at this point, but they tried to develop a way for me to do this if I was able to understand what they were saying to me.

It was a simple thing, and one you may have heard about. If I was asked a question of some kind, I was asked to blink my eyes to answer them: once for yes, twice for no. They asked if I understood this. I did not blink. I wasn't able to acknowledge their question because I didn't know what they were saying. But the odd part was that I still somehow got the words out about Mark, which we still joke about to this day. Over the next few days, I began to recognize some of what was going on around me, but I couldn't speak well yet. I know that they were consistently poking at my arms, legs, and hands. They would roll something on the bottom of my feet, but I could not feel anything, and I couldn't wiggle my toes when asked to do so. I did begin to understand some of their questions after a few days passed, and at one point I was able to reply by blinking my eyes. It took time for me to do this, but I was eventually able to do it.

Some of the questions they would ask me were about current events, and some were simple things to see how my cognitive functioning was, and whether I had any memory. Other questions that were asked of me were things like, "Do you know where you are at? Do you know your name, where you live, and what day and year it is?" I did not know the answers to these questions. I was asked if I knew who the president of our country was, or if I knew what had happened to me. They said that I had thought I was in a car accident. I am not sure of the time span from this point to when I met my family for the first time. When I met my family, I didn't recognize them at all. I don't remember that moment, but I was told this by my family and my doctors. When my family had seen me for the first time after I woke up, they were told that I could not speak, and if I didn't recognize them, it was normal. My mom said that I had moved my fingers in a way to ask for a pen and paper. When they gave one to me, I wrote down, "Car accident?" This is how I had asked them what happened and said what I thought had happened to me. Between that day and the next time they saw me, things again went blank. When they came back the second time, I could not write and didn't really respond to them at all. It seemed at each point when there was a change for me, I had an initial, brief moment of acknowledgment, and then things went blank again.

Over the next week or so, I was taken out of the intensive care unit and moved to a nursing unit. When I had gone into the hospital, I weighed about 175 pounds; when I was moved to the nursing unit, I was 132 pounds. When I think back to those moments to try to remember, I don't know if what I know was told to me or an actual memory. Part of the brain damage I suffered is what they call post-traumatic amnesia. I also had retrograde amnesia. I had lost my memory from nearly everything as a whole—about my life, my family, my friends, and daily living skills. Everything was gone. No one knew how much I would regain; there was no way of knowing this. Time was the key. This terrified me very much, and I was frightened as to what was going to happen with me from this point on. Not knowing was most scary for me then.

While I was in the nursing unit, I did have visitors from friends and neighbors, but I didn't know them. My mom said that no one took offense by my not knowing or remembering them. They were simply happy to see me alive and doing as well as I was. I still wasn't able to talk very well because speaking was difficult. It was within a week or two that I was transferred to the rehabilitation center at the hospital, known as 5 West. It was there they had begun to do more crucial testing of my skills, memory, and other cognitive functions. It wasn't until several years later that I began to remember some of the things that I went through during this time. To this day, I have no real memory of my past after a certain point. When I became coherent enough to understand things, it was explained to me what had happened: I had fallen backward down my apartment stairs and hit my head on the concrete. Then I laid there for a long time, and I had a severe closed-head injury. I had swelling of the brain and extensive blood clotting on and around my brain. Much of this didn't make much sense to me then, but later it did, after a month or two of therapy. They said that the parts of my brain that were affected were the frontal lobes and the right temporal lobes of the brain. These parts of the brain controlled emotion, thought processing, cognitive functions, and informational intake, as well as feelings, reading, memory, colors, and all the simple tasks one does on a daily basis.

They went on to explain that it would take time to recover, and I should not get frustrated in my therapy. I should be patient and allow them to work with me. To put it in short perspective, I was like a child again, in an adult's body. My cognitive function and ability was equivalent to a five-year-old. It was during this testing phase that I began to realize the magnitude of this and what I was facing.

Over time, as I was exposed to my therapies, I started to become more insecure and frustrated on a daily basis, to the point where it like paralyzed me from attempting my therapy. I didn't want to do anymore; I just wanted to stay in my room. I could not walk, sit up on my own, stand on my own, or feed myself. I wasn't able to tell the difference between a fork, a spoon, or a knife. These tasks seem so simple that one doesn't think about it—until one cannot do it. As the old saying goes, "You don't know what you have or how good you have it, until you lose it or it is taken away from you." My therapy schedule was set up for six times per day and five days each week. I had three one-hour sessions in the morning, and three more one-hour sessions in the afternoon. The focus was physical therapy, occupational therapy, and speech therapy.

My family came to visit me a lot, and friends stopped by. One of the things they were consistently reminded of was they should not be offended or hurt from the fact that I may not know who they were. I became very self-conscious of this and didn't want anyone to see me as I was. I felt embarrassed, humiliated, and ashamed. I was even somewhat afraid of them, because I could not relate or remember anything about them. For the most part, conversations were out of the picture. I eventually was able to slowly say some words, but I stuttered a lot and was choppy in saying things. I couldn't yet make full sentences. When it came to other activities, such as when we would have food at noon, everyone would come out to the lunch area. I absolutely hated doing this. I didn't want people to watch someone feed me, or watch me trying to feed myself. I was very self-conscious of this, especially at the dinner table, with the feeling that they were all staring at me and waiting for me to goof up eating, or not knowing which utensil to use. I would think that they would laugh at me, so I always asked if I could eat in my room.

They did allow me to do this for a while, but later they insisted I eat with the rest of the patients in the lunch area. This was something I had to overcome. I remember an elderly lady sitting behind me during lunch one time, and she wouldn't stop coughing. I got so agitated by this that I just wanted to turn around and say to her, "Shut up!" I asked for one of the nurses to come over to me, and I asked to be excused and told her why. I didn't want to say anything to hurt this lady's feelings. She had a simple cold and that was all, but I didn't know how to adjust to this kind of social interaction at this point.

I found myself looking back on all that had happened, trying to make sense of things. I thought a lot about what happened in the emergency room that night, with the light thing in my car, and I wondered how all of these things happened as they did. Knowing that I had died several times in addition to all this, and also surviving the surgery, I thought to myself, *Why would God leave me here like this?* Twenty-three years old, and I didn't know how to process a simple thing such as a lady coughing from a cold. But during my time there, I became friends with this lady. I still think of her often, and I am so glad I asked to be taken to my room before I said something to hurt her feelings. This was the start of what I believe became my greatest asset in recovery: being able to recognize the limitations I had, and my ability to process my surroundings in order to remove myself from what was going on around me to avoid conflict or agitation. When I had started my therapy sessions, I became aware of my limitations, what I was having to relearn, and how to do them.

Physical therapy was really tough for me. I still weighed about 137 pounds and had lost a lot of muscle weight and strength. I wasn't able to sit up by myself, much less stand. I could not eat or feed myself, and I could not hold a pencil. When they would work with me to use my arms, we would try to play catch with a beach ball. This was very frustrating. Just a few years ago, I was selected to play in the first Wisconsin All-Star Baseball Classic as an infielder and pitcher. Now it took all I had to raise my hands and arms to catch a simple beach ball. When first attempting this, the beach ball would hit me in the face or chest; I just couldn't do it. As time moved on, I began to work with light weights to help build my strength. At the beginning, I wasn't able to do it, but eventually I worked my way up to where I could. I know catching a ball seems so very simple, but this was a big accomplishment for me. I was so excited and proud of it that I wanted anyone who came to visit me to play catch.

Not being able to walk, sit up, or stand was very hard on me; that part wasn't going well yet. They eventually began the process of my trying to walk. We started with small steps. Starting from the therapy table, my therapists would help sit me up and then lift me to a standing position. I needed three therapists to try this. I needed what is called a gait belt, with two people helping me, one on each side, holding me up for balance. One person was in front of me, instructing me on what to do.

The goal was to get my feet to move forward in a step formation. All I could do was slightly lift my knees up, barely lifting my heel off the floor. I wasn't able to take a partial step. When I had gotten into several sessions over a week or so, I had begun to be in a lot of pain. Physically, I wasn't able to do this, and I was so frustrated because it was such a struggle.

My occupational therapy was just as hard, if not harder. I didn't know my numbers, colors, or letters. By now I was aware that I was a district sales manager with a sales team I'd trained and was responsible for. I also knew my age of twenty-three. The more I got into this, the more humiliated I felt. I felt like a small child again, having to learn these very simple things all over again. With words such as cat, house, and dog, sometimes I would break down and cry. I didn't want go through this anymore. I remember this puzzle I had to do. It was a board with different shaped objects, and I would have to dump these objects onto the table and put them back in their original places. There were about twenty shapes: circles, triangles, squares, stars, and so on. When I first started doing this, it took me nearly two weeks to put those twenty or so objects back onto the board. Having occupational therapy twice a day for an hour each time and five days each week shows how slow this progress was. I can now do that same board puzzle in about thirty seconds.

Speech therapy was worse yet. I don't mean to overstate this phrase, but each one of these therapy phases was so awful in its own way. I felt like a dummy, and if anyone knew this about me, I thought they would laugh at me and not want to be around me. At the end of each day, I was so exhausted and frustrated on how things were going that I would lie in my bed at night and cry. I could have sat up in my wheelchair with others on the floor, or I could have watched some television. It wasn't self-pity for what I was going through—or maybe it was, to some extent. I simply couldn't comprehend this. I didn't comprehend all that was going on with me, and I couldn't adjust to what I all needed to do. I had a nurse who would come in and sit with me at night, and she'd hold my hand while I lay there and cry. I would ask her why this happened to me. She was so patient and kind to me. I will never forget her name or how many times she had did this with me. I would ask her why I didn't die in the fall, and I would say to her that I now wish that I had died. I didn't want this anymore.

She would say things like, "Sometimes things happen for a reason. There is often no real explanation for why." She would remind me of where I'd been when I first came to the rehab unit, and how far I had come. Some nights she would come in and sit with me even though I would not say anything, and she would simply hold my hand. She was an amazing person.

My family came down many times, and many of those times I didn't speak much to them. They hung out and still talked with me. The rehab unit had a nice pool table in the rec room. About a month after being in the rehab unit, I still wasn't able to walk or stand up on my own yet, but my brother Randy asked me if I would like to try a game of pool. We ended up going to the rec room to give it a try. I could shoot at the balls from my wheelchair, but my brother would ask me to say the number and the color of the ball before I could shoot at it. If I didn't know it, I couldn't shoot at it. Those were the rules he made for us, and he would have to do the same. It was a clever little way to interact with me and help me at the same time. At first I needed help from him, but after a few more weeks of rehab, I was able do a little better at it. I tell him now that he did that because it was the only time and the only way he could beat me on the pool table; he was just taking advantage of my situation. We now kid about it, and it's something we still smack talk about to each other when we play a game of pool.

My boss Mark, whom I had worked with, was very close to me and came down to see me often, nearly every day. He could see the frustration I had, and that I was getting very negative on my progress. He felt I was losing hope. He brought me some things for my room, which included motivational signs that we would use to train our sales team. These were called PMA signs, for "Positive Mental Attitude." The signs would have slogans such as:

- "Keep your mind on the things you want ... and off the things you don't want!"
- Every adversity has a seed of ad equivalent or greater benefit!
- Anything in life worth having is worth working for.
- Do it now!
- If there's nothing to lose by trying, and everything to gain if successful, by all means try with PMA!

One of the other things that Mark had brought down for me was a simple gesture, which I later found out by accident. One on my nurses told me that there was a roll of Life Savers on my night stand next to my bed. I had never noticed them till she told me this. I later learned that Mark had brought those down for me and placed them there. I said to him that I wasn't able to eat them or have them in my mouth, for fear of choking. He said that he was aware of that, but Life Savers were meant to save lives, and he wanted me have all the help I could get so I could pull through this. Now he jokes with me that it was the roll of Life Savers that saved my life, and I should be indebted to him forever. He was kidding of course, but that is the kind of relationship we had: always trying to find an angle to get one up on the other. These motivational signs eventually became part of my daily therapy routine over the next several months. My nurses would read them to me because I wasn't able to read very well yet. Eventually I was able to read them myself. This signage played a significant role in my recovery during this period of time. I truly believe that if Mark had not brought these to my room, my outlook and approach to my recovery process would have taken longer than it did, or I may not have recovered as well. I really do believe this. They helped keep me focused, positive, and motivated to set and reach my therapy goals, which also benefited me in my overall recovery. Once a goal is achieved, it no longer motivates, so I was always adding to my goal list of things I needed to do, and my recovery seemed to move forward again. It was like a momentum shift in a football game. Though it wasn't easy by any means, it kept me grounded and forced me to meet one goal at a time. I refused to get frustrated by trying to do it all at once. I had to approach this with just one tiny step at a time.

One of the things that was very surprising and had impressed the staff was my ability to draw. When I was able to hold a pencil firmly enough, I started doodling and making scribbles. Soon after, I was actually drawing. What was weird about this was I was not able to write my name or words, but I was able to draw. It was picture of a bird with some flowers, which was from one of the get-well cards I had received.

I still have this very first picture I drew; it is one of the photos have included. In late November or early December, the hospital and the clinic was having a Christmas decorating contest. This included all of the hospital floors, the different units, and the offices. The nurses asked me if I would like to make the decoration for the 5 West rehab unit. I said I would give it a go. The idea was to make a nativity scene of some sort. They saw how my drawing was and thought it would be nice to draw the nativity scene. I had asked for a nativity scene or photo of it. I wasn't able to simply draw it; I needed to view it visually. They got some clear window clings that were about two inches in height. I started to freehand each window cling to a two-foot image. It took me a while, but I did complete it, and it was put on the wall in the lounge and dining area. The judging of all the Christmas decorations and scenes were done throughout the entire facility. and the winner was ... 5 West. Everyone was happy for me. To this day, the hospital puts it up every year. Even years later after I had left, whenever I stopped by to visit the unit and say hi to everyone, they would say, "This is the one who drew the nativity scene." That is very cool.

Being able to draw like this helped my focus to detail, and it tunnel-visioned me on each thing I tried to do. If it took me longer to relearn something, that was okay as long as I had every little detail covered. When it came to the retraining my brain to compensate for the losses I had, it seemed less frustrating for me, which was a good thing.

There was one more thing during this time that played a vital role in all this: the company I was working for when this happened, Combined Insurance Company of America, had reassured me that my job and the position I'd held would not be compromised. It would be there waiting for me for as long as it took for me to come back from this. They made this promise to me and my family. Knowing this took a tremendous amount of pressure from me. There are not many companies in today's job market willing to do this, much less make the commitment so early on without knowing how long this was going to take. The importance of this I will share a bit later.

I was admitted to the emergency room and trauma center on September 1, 1990, and I was discharged on December 14. It was just under four months that I had been in the hospital, and it was the best Christmas present my family could have hoped for, to have me home. To use a baseball analogy, I was only just getting out of the batter's box and heading toward first; I had a long ways to go before I could cross home plate. Just to give you an idea of one huge score for me, in 1993 I was selected as the hospital's patient of the year for National Rehabilitation Week. I was interviewed by our local CBS, ABC, and NBC television stations, and by the *Marshfield New Herald*. If you take the thousands and thousands of people they see each year as a whole, to be one of ten individuals over the span of one decade (one selected for each year) is something special to me. It reminds me of how very blessed and fortunate I am.

Chapter 9

Destination Unknown

Upon being discharged from the hospital, there were several options available for me and my family. One of those options was to have me transferred to a special rehabilitation facility in Milwaukee. This rehab facility specialized in helping severe trauma patients relearn the daily activities necessary to reenter society. They'd help me set up routines and learn to adjust to my home, apartment, or assisted living center. I was in fact already scheduled and authorized through my insurance company to be admitted there for one month, which was a good thing. The downside to this was that it very well could have taken me this entire month to adjust to the facility and the staff members who would be working with me. I really didn't want to spend another one or two months in another hospital unit. I didn't have the ability to trust anyone enough, and I was unable to adjust to my surroundings very well. Doing this again could have set me back further and delayed any progress that I'd made up to this point. This was a major point of concern for my family, but if it was best for me, then that was a viable option of choice. My physicians had talked at great length with my family about other alternatives, which included going to a nursing home facility to maintain my speech, occupational, and physical therapy. Another option was to find a rehab facility closer to my parents' home, but that would bring us back to the same issue of adjustment. The other alternative was to keep me working with those I have been working with over the past four months. The only sticking point was to get me to

Marshfield the number of days each week to make my time and rehab effective. By doing this, I would not have to adjust to new nurses, therapists, or doctors.

The Marshfield rehab unit was also near completion of what could be referred to as a mock training street for patients who needed this kind of help. Simply put, it was a corridor that was about three times the width of a usual hospital hallway. It consisted of different living scenarios that would represent everyday activities. There was a bank with a teller booth to relearn and teach me how to enter my bank to handle my finances. There was a grocery store and checkout line to reteach me how to go to the store, shop for some items, and move through the checkout line. It also had half a car, which would allow me to get familiar with a vehicle again. It was a really nice setup, but it was not quite what would have been available to me in Milwaukee. Marshfield also had an apartment room on the rehab unit. Here they began to teach me how to get up on my own, make my own bed, and make breakfast. I relearned to groom myself, brush my teeth, shower, and safely navigate around an apartment, which included how to safely use a stove. My family decided to stay with the staff at the Marshfield hospital and work out a plan to have me brought down three days each week for six to eight hours per day. This would replicate a near similar rehab schedule that I was familiar with when I was there as an inpatient. I learned of my upcoming discharge about two weeks before it was going to happen. I had just learned how to stand up on my own, hold my balance, and take several steps on my own. The next two weeks were about preparing me to leave, working more on consistent balance and stable walking. This would also give my parents more than enough time to prepare my room at their home, and to make any necessary adjustments to their house. My family also needed this time to work out a schedule to bring me back and forth to Marshfield, which was about one hour fifteen minutes from Westboro. I was already comfortable with riding in a vehicle because of the daily and weekend passes I was able to do.

A few months earlier, when I couldn't walk or stand on my own, I was able to go home for a day as things progressed for me. It started with just going for a drive. Then when I was ready for the next step, my family was able to take me to their home for a day. They would pick me up on a Saturday morning and then bring me back that evening. Later, if approved by my parents, a close friend was able to pick me up and take me out for a short drive, and even to a restaurant in the evening for supper. However they had to learn a little bit on how to use the gait belt, and how to hold me when I walked with them. The first outing I had outside of my family taking me was with my friends Dick and Teri Iverson to Pizza Hut. This was close to the hospital and made for a nice little drive. This helped in the decision that was made, because I had no fear of traveling in a car.

When people became aware of my discharge, many friends of mine called my parents and brothers to ask if there was anything they could do. Even some people from town I did not expect offered to help. A schedule was set up so that each family member would take a day from work and drive me on certain days. Then they'd fill the other days with friends and neighbors from my home area who offered to help. My youngest brother was a junior at Rib Lake High School. The principal of our high school at the time, Ray Parks, worked very closely with my parents to allow Rodney to take time away from school so that he could drive me to Marshfield on certain days. Rodney was also able to miss a day of school to be at home with me on certain days if that were needed. My mom was okay with this as long as Rodney kept his grades in good standing. My mom had later explained to me how Ray Parks worked with the family to accommodate any circumstance that would come up, even if it was a last-minute scenario. Mr. Parks had said to my parents that if there was anything they needed help with from his end, they shouldn't hesitate to ask, and he would do all he could to help me and the family. This is one of the true advantages of living in a small community: people reach out and come together in times such as this. Ray is now retired and lives with his wife just down the street from my home. I appreciate that he granted me permission to share his role in my story.

The schedule was setup and had to be maintained for another six months or so. To me, it was unbelievable to see how many of my friends and others stepped up to help me and my family during this period. It removed a huge burden and took a lot of pressure off of them. Even though it may have been an inconvenience to these people, they never grumbled and were happy to do this for me and my family. Everyone said that they would maintain this schedule for as long as it took. I recently found the original list of people who were signed up to take me on those designated days. To this day, I still think of all those individuals and families for what they had done. It truly means a great deal to me.

When the two weeks has passed and I was to be discharged, another challenge surfaced: I didn't want to leave. It is hard to explain this in a way that would make good sense of it, but in my mind at the time, the hospital and the staff was my family and my home. Even though I had gone on some weekend passes with my family, I always referred to the hospital as my home. Whenever it was time for me to go back from being on a weekend pass, I would always ask who was going to take me home, or I would ask how long before I could go home. So when it came for me to be discharged, my thoughts were, *Why would the hospital turn me over to strangers whom I really didn't know or trust?* On the day I was to be discharged, I was so terrified of leaving that I would close my door and not come out of my room, and I would not pack my things to leave. I even went as far as going to another part of the floor to try to hide, but they always tracked me down. I had asked one of my nurses why they would not want me here anymore; I insisted the hospital was my home. I don't know these people I was going to live with, and I cried. I know it may seem as though I was a crybaby through all this, but the emotional toll of everything was so overwhelming for me to deal with, and besides that, I didn't know *how* to deal with it.

The nurse explained to me that these people were my family, and they were now going to help take care of me because I was able to stand up without assistance and walk. I would be coming back three times a week to see the staff and continue to work on my therapy as we had over the last four months. This went on for the entire morning and overlapped into some of the afternoon. They brought my mom in, and we talked together for a little bit. My doctor was asked to come talk to me too. All I could think about was, *What am I going to do without these people whom I have been with for nearly four months?* It was like they had re-raised me from being a child. They were the ones who'd taught me everything I could do up to this point.

My doctor and nurse left to give a few moments for my mom to talk with me. I said to her that I was sorry that I didn't want to leave with her, that I didn't want to live with them. We were both tearful, and she explained to me that no one was going to hurt me or harm me in any way, and they had made the necessary arrangements for me to come back here three times a week for as long as it took to walk better and learn all the things I needed to learn, so that I could someday be on my own again. My mom also explained that I would have my own room for all the privacy I wanted and needed. She asked me to trust them and give them a chance. I said I didn't know if I could do that. She said that she, my dad, my brothers, my sister in-law, and others would understand and be there for me every minute of the day if needed. I looked over to my doctor and my nurse, who were standing just outside the door way. My doctor gave me a wink and a nod, and my nurse gave me a warm smile, as if to say, "It's okay, Ted. You can trust them."

There was a long pause. It seemed like an hour, but was only about ten minutes. No one said a word. Mom then gave me a hug and asked me if I was ready to come home. I had started to cry a little more, but I said okay. I was so torn in my heart and in my mind. I did not want to go, and yet knew that I had to. When I had finally finished packing and was leaving, we went past the nurse's station, and all the staff on the floor presented me with a cake and balloons. On the cake were little baseball figures that made up the infield of a baseball team, assembled and in the position of a team. There was a pitcher, a catcher, and infielders. It was really cool. It was all planned out of course, because everyone knew that I was going home. We gave each other hugs, and they told me to remember we were still a team. I still have those little player figures to this day, displayed in my hutch at my home.

I didn't say much that day on the way to my parents' home where I was going to be staying, but I remember thinking during the drive about how I was going to make it there on my own now. I wasn't going to be alone, but it was a feeling of abandonment from those I had trusted and lived with for so long, even though I knew that was not what they were doing. But it was the next phase of the script laid out for me, and I knew that I would see them again soon. I knew that God had gotten me this far and I couldn't think of a legitimate reason why he would turn his back on me now—not after all the hard work and the anguish it took to bring me to this point. He let me survive this for a reason and had given me several gifts of life. It was now time for me to take the next big step of this journey. I believed he was in my corner and on my side with me for the long haul.

I was scheduled for another surgery in March of 1991, to insert an acrylic plate in my head to replace the part of the skull which they had removed from the first surgery. They needed for the swelling to completely reduce and for all clotting to be out. With that said, what I didn't realize was that the easy part was now behind me. The true struggle had not yet even begun.

Chapter 10

Reflection

To try to answer my earlier question to myself—"Why would God leave me here like this?"—this is what I feel in my heart. I believe that God in fact played a part at every single crossroad I had throughout this ordeal. I believe he placed one of his angels with me to keep me alive for those two and a half hours until I was found. There is no other conceivable medical reason I should have survived all that time, lying unconscious on the ground. That is unheard of with any severe injury to the brain. I believe he guided my friends to turn into my driveway, and he used the dome light in my car as a way to signal them, leading to a reason for them to stop. I truly believe that the light they saw in my car was not the dome light, but the light of an angel that was placed by God. It was the signal for my friends to stop, because there was no mechanical reason for my light to be on. I also believe that he placed an angel with me in the ambulance and did not allow me to die those four separate times. God wanted me survive the fall, the time I was lying there until I was found, and everything that happened during my trip to both hospitals. All that so he could be there for me later on, to hold my hand and settle me down when that time had come. He wanted to prepare and place me in a state of peace in preparation for surgery.

I also believe that he guided my family's hearts, and my mother's heart, which helped them make the right decision with the surgery. I definitely believe that God was the one who took my hand when I was in the emergency room that night. I believe it was his way of letting me know that things would be okay and that he was there for me. He then lifted me so that I could see the reality of what was, and he let me stay here because he had a plan for me. He knew of something in my future that he needed me to do or wanted me to be a part of; it would take years for me to figure it out. I also believe he wanted me to see what the true circumstances were for me and for my family, and he wanted me to know that it would not be an easy task ahead of me.

It was going to be a long, rough road, but God knew that I could do it, was prepared for it, and could come out a better person because of it. God gave me a second chance. In fact, he gave me five changes in all. I believe that he took my hand that night and brought me to a crossroads. I would even consider it my crossover point. I really don't know of any other way to explain this. If there was a reason he left me here, and there was something I was to be a part of, then I had to do my part and do everything possible to overcome what was to be the biggest struggle of my life. I knew that I had a very, very long and rough road ahead of me. As I had once done before, I had to realign my goals and take full advantage of this new, challenging opportunity I had in front of me. It has taken me over ten years to get to what is called my peak.

My peak would be considered the time when my progressing recovery has slowed down or ended. I had always hoped that things would get better, even if it was at a slower pace, but the chances of my getting any better than I am now are slim to none. Simply put, I reached the point where I would get as far as I was going to realistically get, from a recovery standpoint. No one had ever dreamed or imagined that I would have made the recovery I had. God did, though, and he felt that I was ready for the journey. However, what was yet to come after leaving the hospital was a lot tougher and more a struggle than all the months I spent in the hospital. I had to learn life all over again and try to find a way to fit back in. My life as I knew it was over, and starting this new life was not going to be easy. I trusted that God had the right people in the right place and at the right time. He also later brought someone new into my life, and this person became my friend, my mentor, and my lifeline outside of my medical circle. If not for all these incredible people, things would have turned out completely different for me. I have so much respect for all of those who were there for me. I am so grateful and thankful for everything that was done.

All the pieces were now in place, and all the right players were in position. I had a new job to do now, which was to recover the best I could from this and not give up. Again, to use a little baseball verbiage, I had only just got out of the batter's box and I was heading toward first base. As in baseball, you won't always hit the home run. It often requires the help of your teammates to advance you around the bases until you cross home plate to score. I had an amazing team that helped advance me to each base. I did eventually cross home plate to score. Over the years, I have scored in so many different ways. I look forward to sharing that part of my story with you as well. But I can tell you that this new life of mine includes the two most wonderful, precious little girls I could have ever wished for, Zoei and Kylee.

Zoei will turn twelve years old this year, and Kylee just turned nine. My daughters are now old enough to understand some of the things that happened, and they are the brightest part of me. They often ask questions, and I do my best to answer them as best as I can. It was only a few months ago that Kylee asked, "Dad, with all that had happened to you, what would happen if you had to go through all that again? Would you if you knew how it would turn out for you?"

I thought, *Wow, that's a loaded question.* I asked, "Where did that come from?" We were playing a board game on the living room floor, and this question popped out of nowhere.

She said, "Well, I don't know. I was just wondering." I very simply said to her that yes, I absolutely would. Zoei then asked, "Why would you? Wouldn't you be scared?" It almost seemed like they had discussed this with one another at some point, because it was such a serious question and was different than the ones they usually asked.

I told them that I believed things always happened for a reason, and I went on to explained that yes, I would go through all that again. As much I as would hate it and as scared as I would be, knowing that God was to bring the two of them into my life would make it worth it. I commented, "If you really think about it, if none of this would happened to me, the three of us wouldn't be here right now playing this board game—and I wouldn't change that for anything. Does that make any sense? I love you, girls." We gave each other a weird little smile and a hug.

They said, "Thanks, Dad. We love you too." We then went on to finish our board game. This was a very touching and proud moment for me as their dad. I could tell that it meant a lot to them as well.

Outstanding hurler

Rib Lake's Ted Goodrich hurls the ball toward the plate in this action from last week's subregional baseball game between Gilman and the Redmen. The junior hurler moved his record to 6-0 with the win. He allowed just three hits in the 6-1 victory.

(Staff photo by Brian Hallgren)

1984 regional playoffs – Junior year

...ers in the sixth frame to final outcome.
...four-bagger, Slagoski hit Judnic added a two run ...m and Buddy Donaldson ...men 17-hit attack with

Ted Goodrich wasn't happy when he had to face batters with men on base. The young hurler fortunately for the Redmen was up to the task as he shutout a tough Flambeau squad last Tuesday in being a big factor in taking his team to sectional competition.

1985 sectional playoffs - Senior year

1985 Selected to Wisconsin State All Star Game – accepting donation from Pep Simek and Tombstone Pizza to help cover expenses

Myself and Mark Nelson / My District Manager

Insurance Sales awards and trophies prior to injury

My 1987 Chevrolet Camaro

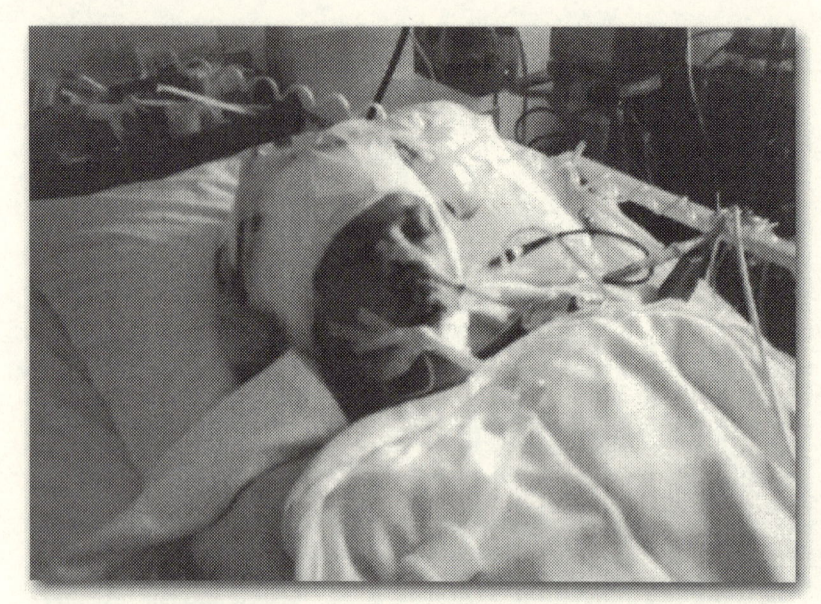

Following initial surgery – First day of coma

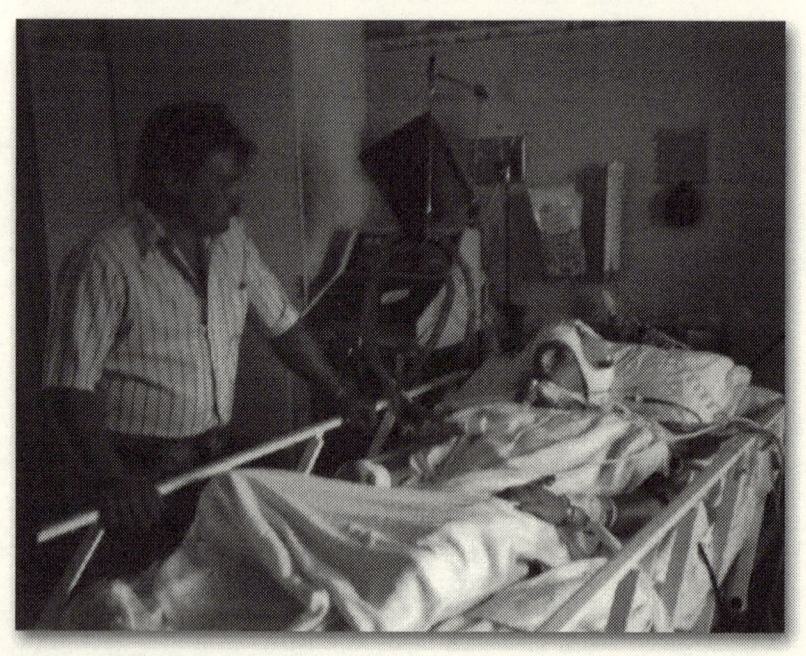

My older brother Conrad spending time with me

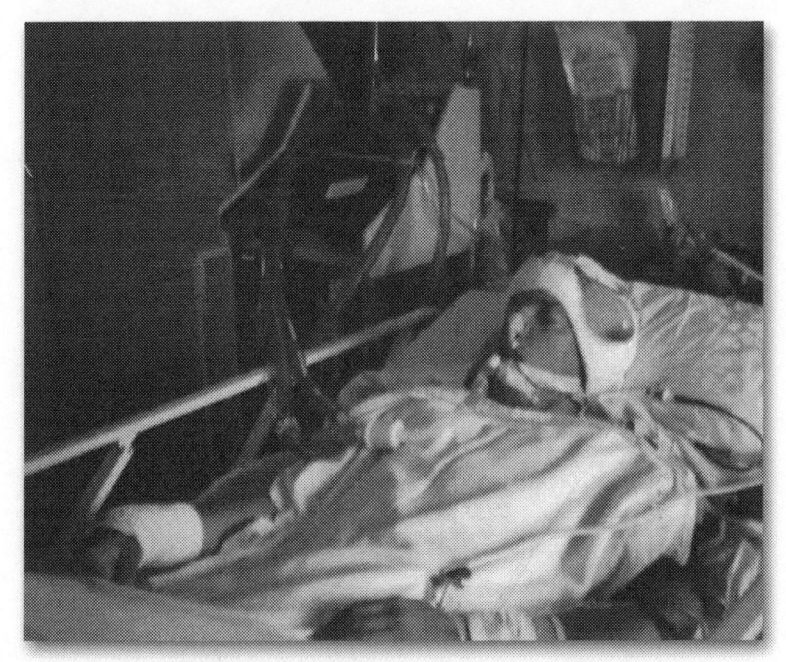

No change after one week had passed

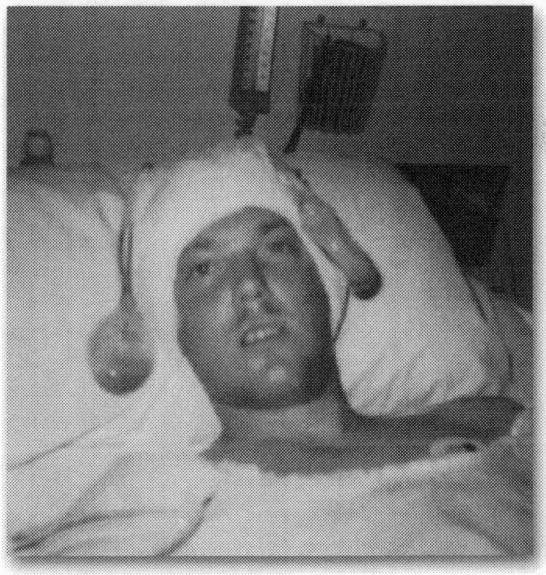

Awakened from coma and life support was removed

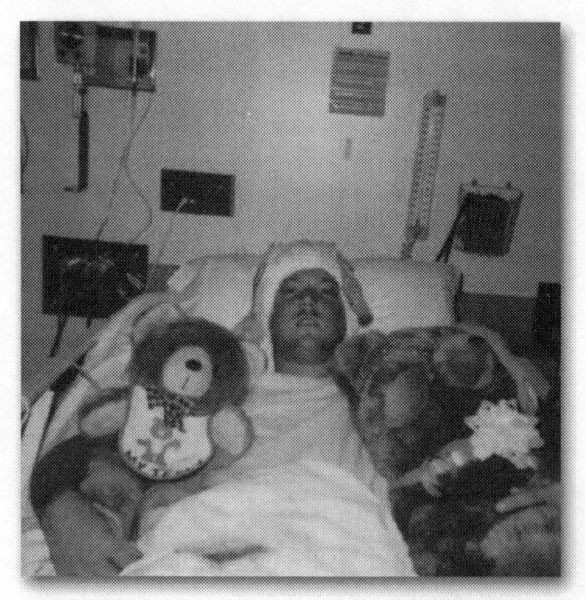

A couple of days after I woke up – with get well gifts

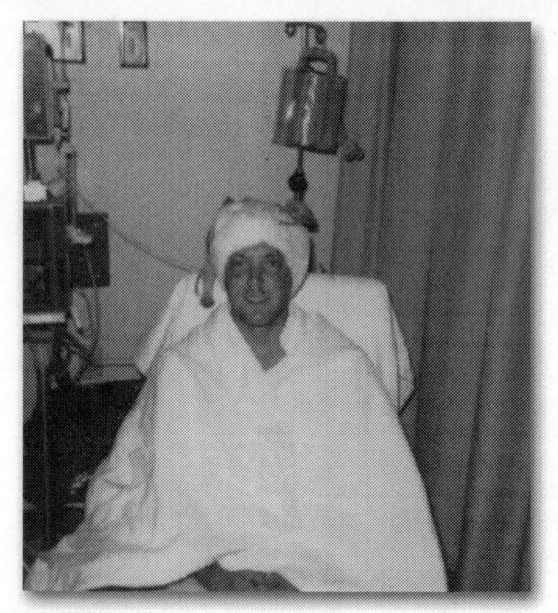

First time sitting up in a chair –
I was propped up underneath my blanket

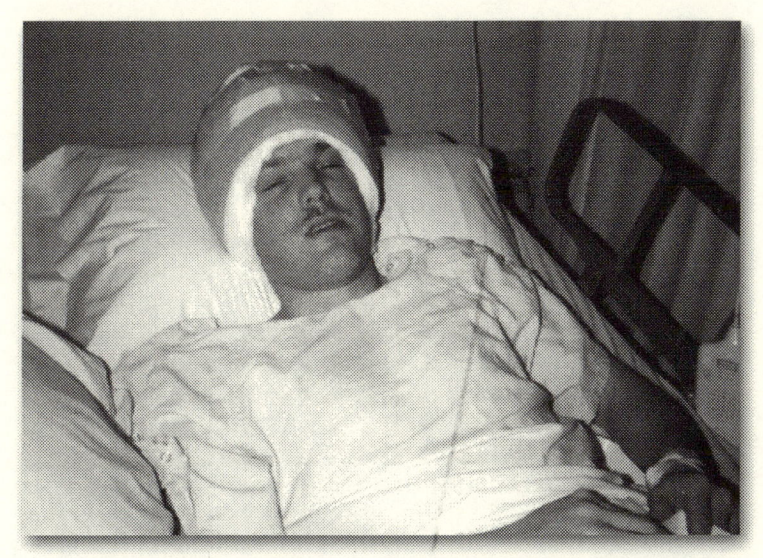

After second surgery in March of 1991 to have a plate put in my head

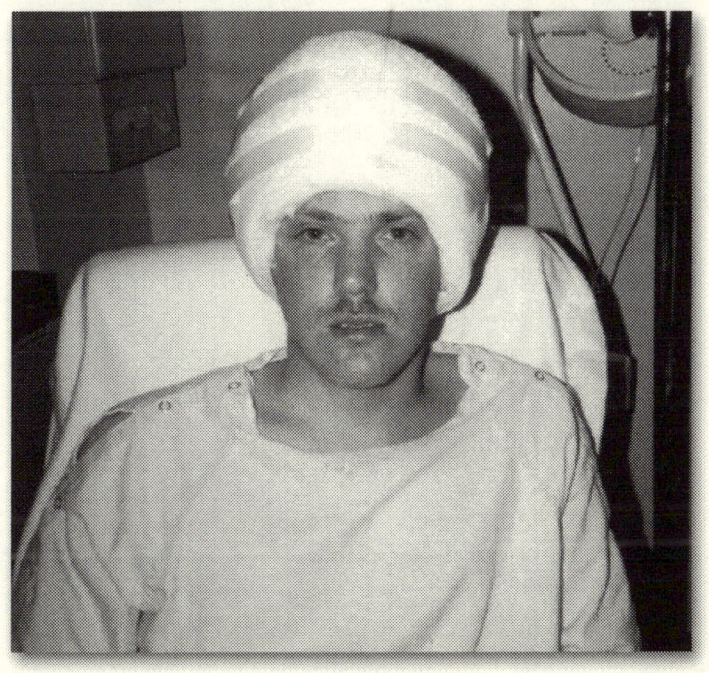

Second surgery in 1991

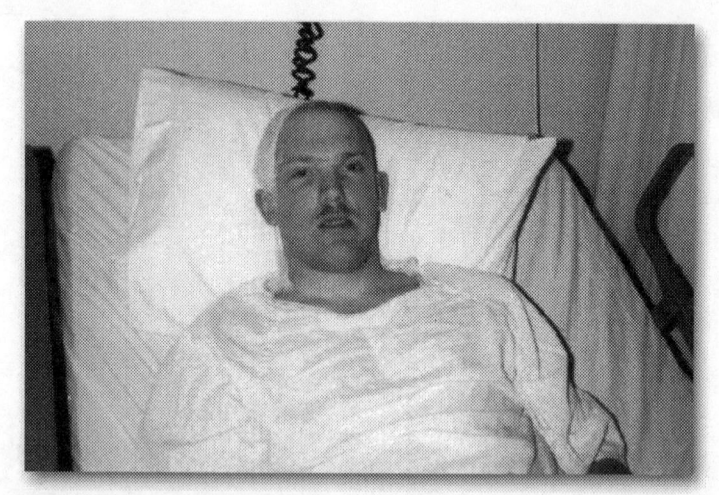

A few months after my first surgery – suction tubes are removed

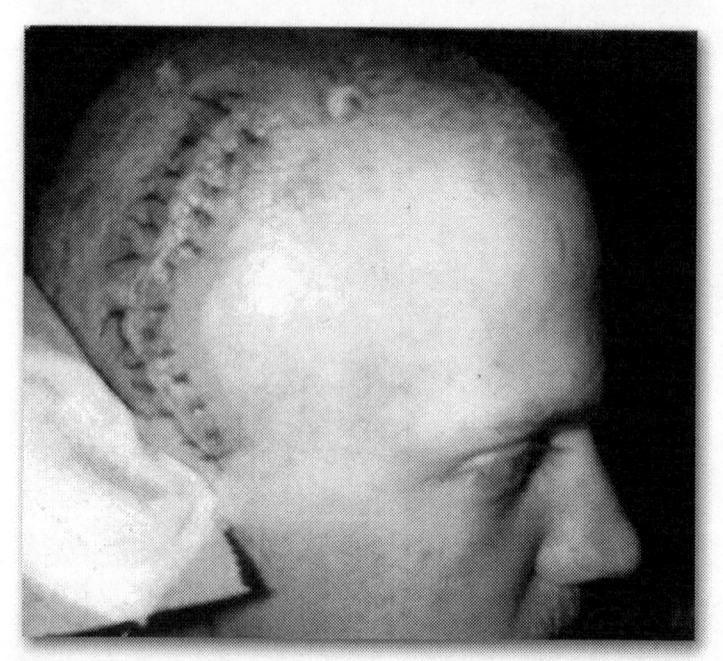

Photo of my surgical insertion and burr holes
taken at home after my second surgery

Hospital room door with P.M.A. signs and photos

A get well card which I had received

A drawing I was able to do even though
I was unable to write letters or numbers

Nativity scene I drew for the hospital Christmas contest

Dedication

I am now forty-six years old, and I have two beautiful little girls. They are the focus of my life and I treasure them every day. However, they were not part of what had happened to me so many years ago. They are now old enough to understand things, and once in a while they have questions. They will learn more of this as they grow older, but if they don't, that's okay too. It's what happens now and in the future that is most important for them to know.

My family is a completely different story. They were smack dab in the middle of all this. As I had mentioned earlier, I do not believe that the patient is always the one who hurts the most or is in the most pain when something like this happens. Your family is right there watching all of this unfold and is probably in just as much or even more pain than you are. I say this because of the helplessness they felt when having to witness such a horrific event, especially for Mom and Dad. There is so much more behind the scenes to speak of that I myself may never know all there is to know. But the emotional shock and the trauma they went through is something not many could bear. If this was one of my children, I don't know how well I could handle something like this. It took a lot of love, courage, and faith to hold as strong as they did.

Families need to know that for someone who has suffered something such as a traumatic brain injury, it is a very long, slow, and tedious process that cannot be forced or rushed. Retraining the brain can take a very long time. I needed to find alternative ways to compensate for what was damaged or lost so that I can accomplish the same or similar results. Mom and Dad and the rest of my family had to adjust to this new life of mine as well. It was something we had to learn together. Not to underscore the effect this had with each family member, but the brunt of this had fallen onto the shoulders of my mom. I could list many of the attributes that she had to endure to get herself through this and yet still be there for the rest of the family. In fact, I will list some of them as I saw it: acceptance, acknowledgment, guts, strong will, courage, love, faith, belief, trust, sacrifice, patience, determination, caring, hope, shock, trauma, endurance, and stamina. The list could go on and on.

She had to be strong for everyone. She had to make the tough decisions and have enough strength for all of us to survive this. She also had the pressures of keeping focused on her job and going to work every day. When I didn't want to leave with her and my dad on that December day in 1990, she knew what I was going through and was prepared for it as much as she possibly could be. I didn't know them or remember them, and I wasn't able to trust them. As hard as this must have been for her, she understood that it was not a purposeful hurt I was inflicting on her. After everything she had gone through with me, for me to say to her that I didn't want to leave with them and couldn't trust them had to be like thrusting a knife into her heart. As she had done many times already, she understood the reality of this and accepted it. She didn't know whether things would ever change or not, and it would have been so easy for her to have placed me in a nursing home or an assisted living center until I had completed my recovery more, but she did not do that.

To this day, I still don't remember everything about them or my family as a son or a brother should, and I probably don't tell them enough how much they mean to me. Logically I know and understand who they are. They are my mom, my dad Russ, and my brothers Conrad, Randy, and Rodney. But emotionally, I am not able to get to where a son or brother should be. I am locked out of that emotion, and it is very difficult to explain, much less understand. I know it is hard for them, and I know that this hurts Mom. I sincerely love them and appreciate every sacrifice they have made for me. I hope and pray that they understand that I don't take them for granted, I have not forgotten all the little things Mom did for me, and I appreciate the things I don't remember her doing for me. She gives me a hug every time she sees me, as she does with all my brothers, even when I probably didn't deserve one. She always says, "You are never too old to let your mom give you a hug." It is with great love, thankfulness, and appreciation that I dedicate this part of my story to one of God's true earthly angels, my mother, Marlene Zimmerman!

My mom and dad

Part Two

Introduction

In today's world, there are many words and phrases that people can say or quote. Some are intended to be negative, and some are intended to be positive. I tend to favor the positive. A quote can be one of optimism, or it can be one of pessimism. I prefer one's of optimism. A person may also look at his life as a glass half full, or a glass half empty. I look at it as half full. A couple of phrases most common are "One man's trash is another man's treasure" and "Beauty is in the eyes of the beholder." Beauty itself can be so many different things to different people. Beauty can be in the form of a shape, a color, a smell, a taste, or a combination of these things. Beauty can also be something that is right in front of you, or a glimpse into one's own imagination or a combination of both.

The same can be true when asked to define the word treasure. What is treasure, and what does it mean to you? What is beauty, and what does that mean to you? In my own life, I can say that I have experienced many treasures. But when recovering from a catastrophic injury such as the one I had experienced with my traumatic brain injury, the question now is, how do I find something beautiful again after something so devastating has occurred? There is much natural beauty in the world to look at every day. There is also much natural disaster that can happen on any given day. In the part of the country where I live, in Wisconsin, one of those natural disasters that comes to mind is a thunderstorm. Thunderstorms here can happen at any time during the spring, summer, and fall. They can be so severe that they are capable of producing large hail, damaging winds, and tornados, leaving a path of devastation behind, including the loss of life. If something like a tornado should ever occur, and you survive a natural disaster, then as long as you have your life, that is really the bottom line. Material things can be replaced, but a life cannot be.

For me, the beauty I refer to following such a storm comes in the form of a rainbow, a simple, bright ray of colors that appears in the sky, letting you know that the worst has passed or that the storm is over. In general, people do not wake up in the morning and say to themselves, "Gee, I think I'll look for something beautiful today." Some may wake up and look for positive things to happen, such as those who set personal daily goals in their lives or have goal-oriented careers. People of faith may wake up and pray for themselves and for others, to help make the world a better place. The list can go on and on. When it comes to something so simple such as a rainbow, most people would say it is a thing of beauty. It is something you don't have to go out of your way to find. It will simply appear after a soft spring shower or a thunderstorm. A rainbow is also something that can bring a sense of calm to someone after experiencing such a storm, and it can bring a simple smile after a gentle spring shower. It's a simple joy that God has created for us to let us know the storm has passed.

When I had started to heal and recover from this injury, I became aware that I was going to have many storms to weather out. With every storm I faced, whether it was large or small in scale, I had to fight my way through it and find that little rainbow. These little rainbows may have had little to no impact on those around me. In fact, many of these little rainbows went unnoticed by others because my recovery took so many years. But for me, they were the little signs of joy that meant a particular storm I was going through had passed. To this day, I continue to see those little rainbows, sometimes on a daily basis, because I will always continue to weather out a storm in one form or another. The damage to my brain is permanent and irreversible, and the residual effects of that damage is something that I deal with every day of my life. My goal of sharing the second half of my journey with you is to help make you aware that no matter how difficult things may be, and no matter how severe your own personal storm may be, there will always be some hope in the form of your own little rainbow to let you know that things will be okay. It will be a little brighter for you in the end. It doesn't take much effort for someone to be negative or look for the negative in his life. That is easy, and anybody can do that. However, it does take a lot of effort and hard work to be positive and stay motivated, even when there are times you don't feel that way. Not everyone can do that. The perception that one has of oneself is the perception one reflects onto others.

Sometimes it only takes that one little speck of hope, that little rainbow, to make all the difference in your life.

Chapter 11

The First Day of the Rest of My Life

When I left the Marshfield hospital with my parents on that day in December, it was a very quiet, long, and lonely ride home. Snow covered the ground, and people had out their Christmas ornaments and decorations. Some homes were beautifully decorated, which gave a little serenity to the drive. Surprisingly, I had noticed some nativity scenes along the way. It made me think of the nativity scene I'd drawn on the unit for the decoration contest, and that brought a little smile to my face. It was about an hour and a half drive to my parents' home, and it gave me a lot of time to think about all the changes that were taking place, and how different things would be for me from this day forward. When I was able to go out on one of my day passes or the weekend pass for visits, I always knew in the back of my mind that I would make my way back to the hospital within a day or two. While on one of these passes, if I wished to leave early, I had the security of knowing that someone was there to drive me back to Marshfield. This time, however, it was going to be different. Whatever happened from this day forward, I would be staying right where I was heading: my parents' home.

This put me into a new way of thinking and changed my method of thought processing. I had lost the security I once had, relying on my reassurance of staying at the hospital. To me, that was like cutting the only lifeline I had to who I was, and where I could go to truly feel safe. My security blanket was gone. During the drive to my new home, I kept taking long, deep breaths to try to relax myself and keep calm.

Along the way, we stopped for lunch—or I should say, we went through a Hardee's drive-through and ate our lunch on the way home. Being around others this day was something my parents knew would be difficult for me, so they did not try to encourage me to take on such a task. As we ate our lunch and drove, my dad started some conversation by asking me how my sandwich and fries were. I was familiar with the drive, but instead I had asked them how far we had to go before we got to the house. I thought if I kept to simple questions with them, I wouldn't be too nervous when we got there. I tried to avoid what I felt were open-ended questions.

I asked them about my room, the days that I would be going back for therapy, and things like that—something that did not include a lot of reply or input from my end. I don't believe that I ever answered my dad's question about my sandwich and fries. I could have said that it was good, and that would have been the end of it. I tried to dodge any questions from them so I wouldn't have to feel like I had to try to explain something.

When we arrived at their home, it seemed as it always had when I was there before. The only difference this time was that there were no other cars parked in the driveway, and there didn't appear to be any other people around. This was good for me so that I didn't have to visit with anyone or have to try to remember things while moving in. In a weird sense, it felt like one would feel when going to a funeral. I felt as though I had to do this out of respect to my parents, for all that they had done for me. It was a somber feeling, and I wasn't looking forward to it. There was a sense of relief that no one was there. I asked if anyone was inside or was maybe coming later. My mom said that it was going to be the three of us today. She asked if that was okay with me, and I said yes, it was. Their idea was to have nothing and no one around to give me any extra pressures or stress while coming home. It was explained by my doctor that this was going to be a tremendous adjustment for me, and less activity going on around me would make it easier for me to focus on my new, permanent surroundings. It would be in everyone's best interest. My parents wanted to allow me to come home, get familiar with my room, and not have to mingle with anyone around me. This would allow me to settle in at my own pace without multiple distractions.

When I was there for the day or a weekend on one of my passes, I would spend much of my time within one or two places in the house; I would keep my space confined and concentrated. Now things were different. When we walked through the door, there was a small sign that read, "Welcome Home, Teddy. We all love you." The radio was playing softly from the living room so that there wasn't dead silence in the house. While my dad was bringing in my suitcase and hospital things from the car, Mom was explaining some of the changes that were made for me. The subtle changes were simple things that would help make it easier for me to navigate my way around the house so that I needed little to no assistance to get something, especially around the kitchen area. Self-independence in any small way was vital for my adjustment. There were no structural changes to the house that needed to be made for me. I think that some of the non-changes I noticed was due to the fact that I was looking at things differently, studying the house in more detail compared to when I was on short visits.

After my dad had all my things brought in, my mom asked if I would like to see my room. It was rearranged a little bit from when I was there on my passes. She said they took some things out to make it more spacey and less congested, to make it easier for me to move around. She asked me if everything looked okay or if there was anything I needed. I said that everything looked wonderful. I noticed the stuffed animals on my bed, which I'd had in my room at the hospital. Seeing those gave me some sense of calm.

They said that they would leave me alone to settle in, put away my clothes, or lie down to rest. I said that the room was nice and thanked them for making it ready for me. I added that I would like to rest for a while and put my clothes away later. They said that was okay and explained that everything in the house was for me to use; I should consider it as my own, and I should not be afraid to ask for something I needed. They would be in the other room. My mom said that she had taken the next three weeks off work to be available for me and help me with whatever I needed, and if I didn't need much help, then we could get to know each other a little better. She asked if that was okay with me, and I said that I appreciated her doing that for me. They both gave me a hug and left to let me settle in. As they were closing the door to leave, they both said that it was nice to have me there with them. I got a little teary eyed, but I honestly don't know if they were tears of joy or of fear. I think there may have been a little of both. Either way, the next phase was about to begin.

Chapter 12

Extent of My Injuries: The Big Picture

After several months of rehabilitation and neuropsycholblical testing, my doctors were able to identify much of the damage that was done to my brain. They already knew the areas of my brain that were damaged, but they were unable to determine the severity of that damage or the long-term effects until more time passed. Time was an exhausting factor in determining how severe this was and how it would play out. The majority of damage was to my frontal lobes, which are located directly in front of the brain, directly behind the forehead area. Secondary damage was done to the right temporal lobe area, which is located on the right side of the brain just above the right ear area; this was the side in which I had received the skull fracture. The medical information I use and paraphrase in this chapter was retrieved through the following brain injury resource websites[1]

---

[1]
References

   www.braininjury.com;
   www.brainandspinalcord.org;
   www.traumaticbraininjury.com;
   www.neuroskills.com;

Frontal lobe injuries are described as follows: The frontal lobes provide the integration of all other brain functions into a seamless whole. Planning, multitasking, risk assessment and the exquisite complexities of social interaction are all handled by the frontal lobes. Because of their location, the frontal lobes are often first to be injured in traumatic events. The lobes can be pushed forward into the bony ridges in the front of the skull, resulting in bruising and tearing. Thousands of studies have been done over the years and it is now known that the notion of one's "self" resides largely in the frontal lobes. Therefore, a frontal lobe injury in a very true sense, changes an individual from their former self to a new person, and in the vast majority of cases, an inferior person. A couple of things tend to be true for individuals with frontal lobe injuries. Disinhibition can occur, which means the individual lacks the screening device that keeps them from saying what's on their mind. This can create problems within the workplace and in social settings.

Multitasking becomes almost impossible. The frontal lobe allows us to juggle and prioritize things, and that is extraordinarily difficult with this type of injury.

Initiating activity becomes more difficult; people with this injury often are described as being "in idle" until they are prompted to do what used to be normal activities for them. Social awkwardness is almost universally noted; this is because the frontal lobe is the part of the brain that deciphers the many nuance complexities of interacting with people. We take it for granted, but there are many, many clues visual, auditory and positional that have to be integrated into dealing with people in almost any way. People with frontal lobe injury are often described as "off rhythm" or "a step behind" in conversations. A frontal lobe injury will also diminish the cognitive reserve of a victim, making them more likely to face old age dementia at an earlier age and be more vulnerable to Alzheimer's as they age. Cognitive retraining and keeping the brain as busy as possible with the most complex things possible will help it rewire (neuroplasticity) after an injury or accident. When traumatic injuries such as this occur, a medical trauma doctor such as a neurosurgeon will perform a specific test on the individual called the Glasgow Coma Scale. This test is immediately done upon the patient arriving to the trauma center. This is not a test which can be performed in the field or at the scene of the accident. Under an ideal scenario, the test should be done within an hour of the injury. The Glasgow Coma Scale is based on a fifteen-point scale system for estimating and categorizing the outcomes of a brain injury. The basis of the test is on overall social capability or the dependence on others. This is the most commonly used test at trauma centers throughout the country for Traumatic Brain Injuries.

Note: information which I am using to describe this section was researched from TraumaticBrainInjury.Com, LLC. The mission of TraumaticBrainInjury.Com is to be the leading Internet resource for education, advocacy, research and support for brain injury survivors, their families and medical and rehabilitation professionals. How the Glasgow Scale actually works is that it measures the motor response, verbal response, and eye opening response using a fifteen-point scale system. Each category has a set of numbers assigned to determine the level of severity (for example, ten being the best possible outcome, and one being the worst possible outcome). The attending physician will use various methods to test the stimuli in each category and then assign the corresponding number next to it as he or she proceeds through the test.

I. Motor Responsiveness
6 – Obeys commands fully
5 – Localizes to noxious stimuli
4 – Withdraws from noxious stimuli
3 – Abnormal flexion posturing
2 – Extensor response
1 – No response

II. Verbal Responsiveness
5 – Alert and Oriented
4 – Confused, yet coherent, speech
3 – Inappropriate words and jumbled phrases consisting of words;
2 – Incomprehensible sounds;
1 – No sounds.

III. Eye Opening Responsiveness
4 – Spontaneous eye opening;
3 – Eyes open to speech;
2 – Eyes open to pain;
1 – No eye opening.

The score is determined by adding the values of the three categories. This number helps medical practitioners categorize the four possible levels for survival, with a lower number indicating a more severe injury and a poorer prognosis. The following categories are various levels of brain trauma based on the point scale listed above.

Mild brain trauma would be defined with a point rating of 13–15. Moderate brain trauma is defined as a brain injury resulting in a loss of consciousness from 30 minutes to 6 hours and a Glasgow Coma Scale of 9–12. Severe brain injury is defined as a brain injury resulting in a loss of consciousness of greater than 6 hours and a Glasgow Coma Scale of 3–8. Severe TBI symptoms may result in permanent neurobiological damage that can produce lifelong deficits to varying degrees. The impact of a moderate to severe brain injury depends on the following:

1) Severity of initial injury
2) Rate/completeness of physiological recovery
3) Functions affected
4) Meaning of dysfunction to the individual
5) Resources available to aid recovery
6) Areas of function not affected by TBI

This initial method of medical testing upon my arrival at the Marshfield Trauma Center had me at the point level of three on the Glasgow Coma Scale. According to the available resources I have listed above, only about 3 percent of all traumatic brain injuries will endure a epidural hematoma and have the surgical procedure which I had performed. If death does not occur at the time of injury and a patient has a Glasgow scale of 3–4 after 24 hours, 87 percent of those patients will die. About 7 percent will have a moderate to good recovery. The remaining percentage could remain in a vegetative state or have a different result. This will give you a clearer picture of the mess I was in when I had awakened from my coma.

After some time had passed, a series of symptoms began to arise after further detailed testing was able to be completed. The following is a descriptive list of the severe TBI symptoms I had endured as a result of the brain injury to my frontal lobes. These are listed under the different functional areas of the brain.

- Cognitive Deficits: attention, concentration, distractibility, memory, speed of processing and informational intake, confusion, language processing, and executive functions.
- Speech and Language: not understanding spoken word (receptive aphasia), difficulty speaking and being understood (expressive aphasia), slurred speech, speaking very fast or very slow, problems reading, problems writing.
- Sensory: difficulties with interpretation of touch, temperature, movement, limb position, and fine discrimination
- Perceptual: difficulty integrating or patterning of sensory impressions into psychologically meaningful data
- Vision: weakness of eye muscles and double vision (diplopia), blurred vision, intolerance of light (photophobia)
- Hearing: ringing in the ears (tinitus), increased sensitivity to sounds.
- Physical Changes: chronic pain, sleep disorders (circadian rhythm disorder), loss of stamina, appetite changes, regulation of body temperature (cold/heat intolerance)
- Social and Emotional: dependent behaviors, emotional ability, lack of motivation, irritability, depression

The symptom deficits that I had received from the damage to my right temporal lobe was fortunately limited to three out of eight areas of function from this part of the brain: disturbance in selective attention of auditory and visual input, impaired organizational and categorization of verbal material, and impaired long-term factual memory. Between the two areas affected, this is a long list of damaged deficits I was facing when I began my rehabilitation. Some of my deficits listed above have healed to some degree and have gotten better over a period of many years. For many others, I had to go through the process of retraining my brain to learn alternative ways to use that functional area the best I could; this may also be known as brain rewiring. A change this devastating to the brain function can have a dramatic impact on family, job, social, and community interaction. From a rehabilitation standpoint, you can see what kind of challenges I had ahead of me. Some deficits were more severely impacted than others. The brain swelling, blood mass, bruising, scarring, the area of impact, and the length of time I laid before found were factors in overall severity levels. Many of these were managed through months of therapy in the hospital and with medication. After my discharge, things were managed by the hospital on an outpatient basis with many follow-up visits, continued medication, and self-assessments.

It's been twenty-five years now, as I just passed my September 1 anniversary date. I still have many of these deficits, which I deal with on a daily basis. Some are more obvious than others. Some I can manage well, and some I can disguise in my activities so that they are too subtle to notice. But they hinder my life in some form or another every single day. If one were to look at me today, one would never know that anything like this had ever happened to me. I have no visual or physical characteristics that are noticeable by simply looking at me. Sometimes this is often worse than if I were to have visible signs of such an injury, because it is hard for someone to understand when I am unable to do something that seems very simple and so routine. People who know me and know of what happened to me understand this. It took me a long time to outgrow this issue. If I cannot do it, I no longer feel that I have to overexplain to anyone why I can't perform a certain way or feel ashamed of it. I simply do what I can, and if I cannot, I accept it and move on. That is all that I can do.

Chapter 13

Adjusting to My New Home

The first three months or so of staying with my parents had its ups and downs. I was continuing with my days going to Marshfield for my therapy. I always looked forward to my therapy days not so much for the therapy itself but because I was returning to a familiar place, a place of security. I realize that I may refer to this often throughout my story, but there was no place that I could feel comfortable. As far as my adjustment at my parents' home, things did get better for me, but not all at once. My mom would tell me the story that it took nearly three months before I would come out of my room when they were home, or if anyone was there. The whole mingling and visiting thing changed once I had moved in. The only time I really came out was to shower or to use the bathroom, which was across the hall from my room.

When it came to mealtimes, I would not come out. My mom would have a small table in the hallway next to my door. She would knock lightly to let me know that my plate was outside of the door, ready for me to eat. Then I would open my door and bring it into my room. When I was done, I would place the plate back on the table for her or my dad to pick up. They had also made up a menu for me to choose what I wanted to eat for each meal, similar to the menus I was used to choosing to from at the hospital. They would always have that made for me, because that was part of my normal routine. There were times I would eat what they were eating, but I was so used to selecting my meals with a dietitian and from a menu that my parents continued this with me till I passed through that stage. Mom said that this routine also went on for nearly three months. The staff at the hospital explained to them that these routines were very important during the recovery stages from this type of injury. Some of the routines seemed so tedious and were probably very demanding on my parents, but they did it. This shows how much dedication they had to making this work for me. They didn't want me to go to Milwaukee, so they put tremendous effort into doing what was needed.

During this time period, I did come out of my room when they left the house. In order to get me out of my room more, my parents would knock on my door and tell me that they were either going to town to do some shopping, going out to plow snow, or going for a walk. This was to give me an opportunity to come out and go through cabinets, shelves, and things to familiarize myself with the house and learn where things were at. It was when they were home that I spent most of my time in my room. When my mom went back to work, they always had someone checking on me, mostly by telephone. It wasn't till sometime after my second surgery was completed that I slowly began to show more interest in coming out and sitting with my parents, and I was more engaged with other family members. I believe that this had much to do with the success I was having with my therapy sessions. Things from that standpoint began to show more gainful measurements, and my self-confidence progressed.

The biggest jump I had made with this process was when I suddenly came out of my bedroom and walked into the living room one evening. My mom and dad both looked at me like deer in headlights. I asked them if it was all right if I sat and watched television with them. They said of course it was okay. She told me that I would say thank you and would sit down in a chair near the corner of the room. When I did this, they did not try to engage me in conversations or anything; they would simply allow me to sit and watch television with them. They were aware that this was huge for me, and they didn't want to push it too far by making me feel nervous or uncomfortable. That could have regressed me back to staying in my room. It was as though they knew how to handle every step of progress without posing a threat to me that would result in regression. I honestly don't know how they did all of this. They were doing all the right things a family needed to do. That seemed to be the turning point for me, when it came to coming out of my room more and interacting with them more.

My second surgery was scheduled to be performed in March 1991, and it was going to be performed at the Marshfield hospital by the same neurosurgeon who did my original surgery. I remember going through all the pre-op procedures and was completely aware of what was going on and what the surgical procedure was about. My brain had returned to its normal size, the blood mass was not there anymore, and all the swelling was gone. They were going to insert an acrylic plate and attach it to my skull to cover the opening I had from when they'd removed it during the first surgery. The size of the plate would be between a golf ball and a tennis ball in size. An acrylic plate was going to be harder than the skull itself, so no metal was used or needed.

This was better from a technology standpoint and was better for my body overall. It was scary for me from the standpoint that I was awake and aware of going into surgery. I knew it was going to have a good outcome, but I was nervous. I remember them prepping me and attaching all the equipment needed; I talked with the nurses as they were doing this. The nerves really started to kick in when they shaved my head. The neurosurgeon came up to me and said that he was going to enter through the same insertion as before, so that I would not have worry about any new cuts or scarring. He said that my family was waiting outside to see me before we went to the operating room. When I was prepped and ready to go, they wheeled me out on my gurney into the hallway, where my family was waiting. They wished me luck and said not to worry, and they would be here when I woke up. There was even a joke or two going around to lighten the mood. When it was time to go, they wheeled me down the hall. It seemed a little freaky to me. Have you ever watched a movie where someone is being taken to an operating room? All you see when you look up are the lights on the ceiling passing by, and the head of the person pushing you. If you have ever watched a horror movie, it was a crazy guy pushing you on a cart down the hallway into his torture room. These were the thoughts going through my mind at that time.

When I was in the operating room itself, it was very cool in temperature. The doctor asked me if I was comfortable and ready to begin. He again explained to me what the procedure was and how long it could take. Then the hospital chaplain came over to say a prayer with me, and that made me more relaxed, though I was still nervous. I was then asked to start counting backward from one hundred. I remembering counting backward to ninety-six, and I was out. The surgery took about six hours, and everything went according to plan. When I was taken to the recovery room, I was kept for a longer period of time because I became much sicker than they thought I would be coming off of the anesthetic. It was close to an extra two hours that they kept me there as a precaution.

When I woke up and was coherent, I had been moved to the nursing unit. I seemed to have relapsed on some of the symptoms I'd had the first time around with my first surgery. It wasn't a major concern but was somewhat unexpected. I was having some memory issues again, balance issues, and some difficulty on a few cognitive things. This could have been from some of the scarring or the stress of the surgery on those areas of the brain. They kept me for a little over a week; most patients would have been out within four days. I had done some therapy again during that week, but everything worked itself out, and I was discharged to return home. I continued my scheduled therapy for an additional three to four months, at which time I was okay to discontinue and do the rest at home. I did go back on a regular basis for other follow-up visits, and sometimes I went simply to visit the staff at the rehab unit.

Things had been consistently improving for me at this point. There was still a long way to go, but progress was clearly evident.

Chapter 14

Meeting Old Friends as New Friends

One of the next steps I needed to attempt was meeting my friends. I was not able to drive for a minimum of one year, due to the nature of injury. State law required the hospital to literally take possession of my driver's license, so there were limited ways to approach meeting friends. The hospital staff suggested we keep things within my comfort zone and make it as stress-free as possible. If I wasn't ready for such a task, it was not to be pushed or forced upon me.

However, when there was an opportunity to meet one of my friends, my mom would call the person ahead of time and ask if he or she would like to see me. All of my friends said yes, but it started out only one at a time. One of the systems that worked out was a very simple one. My mom usually paid her local bills by the way of mail. She started to pay some of these bills in person. The concept of this was that while she was inside paying a particular bill, a friend of mine and would come up to the car and say hi. They were aware that I most likely would not recognize them, so it would go something like this.

My mom would ask me to ride along, and I would wait in the car while she went in to pay her phone bill. While she was doing this, my buddy, who was the owner of the phone company that sponsored our team, walked out to the car, knowing I was sitting in there. He would walk up to me, and extend his hand, and say, "Hi, Ted. My name is … It's nice to meet you." I would say, "It is nice to meet you." To keep things simple, he talked about what a nice day it was to be out for a drive. I asked him if this was where he worked. He said yes, because he and his dad were owners of the phone company. Of course I'd known all this before, but this was how it was slowly done. We finished talking, and he would say for me to have a nice day and that it was a pleasure meeting me, adding that we'd see one another again soon.

Shortly after he went back in, an older man came walking out; I wasn't sure but assumed it was his dad. He came up to me in the same manner to introduce himself. "Hi, Teddy. It is so nice to see you again." I was nervous talking with them, but it was a big step for me. All the guys were understanding and cool about the way this was being done. It wasn't intimidating or stressful, just some nerves and anxiety.

When things like this were planned, my mom would talk to them ahead of time and let them know where I was at regarding my ability and how much I could handle. Most of my outings were done without me knowing that I was going to actually meet anyone. Whenever this was done, the friend whom I was going to meet would always walk coming from the front of the car, never from the side or the back. This was designed so that I would not be startled, and so that I could visualize them as they approached me. This would give me a chance to see if there was any hint of memory of who they were. They would stop next to the car, I would roll down the window, and they would say hi. I would say hi back. It was always kept to a simple interaction. Sometimes they would say that they happened to see me sitting in the car and wanted to walk over and say hi. Other times they would say that my mom was nearly finished and would be right out. It was only for about five minutes or so, but this was how it all had to start. My mom would then come out and start talking to my friend, which forced me listen to the way they engaged, and then she'd bring me into the conversation. My brothers had worked out the same system when I went with them. It wasn't all of the time, but this was done enough to get me headed in that directional train of thought.

From my standpoint, it was okay. I was able to get out of the house, go for a nice ride, interact with who was taking me, and then meet some of my buddies. The one thing that none of them did was ask me, "Do you remember me? Do you remember things we did together? What do you remember?" They never did that once to me. That line of questioning would have made me very defensive and anxious to the point of agitation, or even bring on a panic attack. I later learned that it was my mom who first made the request for my friends not to ask those kinds of questions. She explained why, and they understood completely. Some of the guys would come right out and ask a member of my family how to approach me so as not to make me feel intimidated. My family was always right on top of these things. They really knew what they were doing when this phase of recovery was attempted. Each time it seemed to get a little bit easier. Later on, if I knew I was about to meet a particular person, I would need to be conditioned ahead of time; a surprise visit was something I didn't know how to handle yet.

One of my good friends whom I had mentioned earlier was Dan Fliehs. He was the one who came down to visit me and tried to find out if I was alive at the hospital the night I got hurt. Due to hospital policy, he was unable to get any information because he was not an immediate family member. My mom called him one day and asked if he would like to come over to the house and visit with me. She explained to him that I was home alone a lot now and was having a hard time of things, and I was getting frustrated. He said, "Of course I would, Marlene. I would love to." My mom wanted to prep me and see if I was up for a visitor at the house like this. She explained to me who he was, how I knew him, and how long I had known him. She also explained to me the Dan was aware that I wouldn't remember him, and he was okay with that. Mom did share with him about how he could best interact with me when he came over. She told him that I liked to shoot pool, and there was a pool table downstairs. I said that I was okay with it, so Dan was invited over. As I was waiting for him to arrive, I was really nervous. I didn't know what to expect or what he would think of me having to live here with my parents, because they had to help take care of me. This time, my parents did encourage me to interact and talk to Dan. "Give it an effort, and see how it goes. He understands and isn't going to laugh or think bad of you," they said to me. This was another huge step for me, to say the least.

When Dan arrived and came through the door, he greeted my mom and dad and then looked over to me. I think he may have been more nervous than I was. He visited with mom and dad for a bit, which allowed me to get my thoughts together. I then made a few steps toward him, and he did the same toward me, extending his hand to shake my hand. He said, "Teddy Goodrich, it is so nice to see you up and around, my friend. You had us all worried there for a while."

This time I didn't say it was nice to meet you. I said, "It is nice to see you again," based on the information my mom told me prior to him getting there.

We stood around, and the four of us chatted about things in general. My dad got us a soda, and then Dan and I sat in the living room and talked a bit.

Dan asked me how I was doing and how things were going for me overall. I was okay with these kinds of questions at this point. He never asked me if I remembered anything and stayed away from that kind of conversation. My talking was still somewhat slow, and my words didn't come out quickly, but it was all good. I explained to him where I was at in my recovery stage and that I'd had my second surgery, which went well. Everything was kept simple and short. At one point he said, "I heard your parents have a pool table downstairs." He asked if I would like to shoot a game or two, and I said sure. I said that I had shot some pool at the hospital rec room with my brothers, but I wasn't very good at it yet. He said, "Wait till you see me try to knock those balls in the pockets. You'll look like a pro compared to me."

We both laughed. My mom had shared with him on the rules I had in place with my brothers Randy and Rodney: I had to say the color and the number of the ball before I could shoot at it. By this time I was doing pretty well with it. I never went downstairs when alone or by myself, for fear of falling. I always needed someone to go with me, and I was aware of that.

Dan later shared with me that before we had gone downstairs that day, I had asked him if I could show him something. He told me, "Yes, of course you can, Teddy." He said that I took him into my room to show him all of my baseball trophies and the other awards I had. He said that I had explained to him I had all of these trophies and things, but I didn't remember receiving them or how I got them. Dan said to me that he and I played a lot of baseball together, and I'd deserved all those awards and trophies. Dan spent about an hour or two with me that day, and I really enjoyed it. I was getting tired after we had played a couple of games, and he could tell.

It's kind of funny now, but Dan said to me months later that there was one point where I was getting a little frustrated because I wasn't making many shots, and I got some of the numbers and colors mixed up. I think it was mostly due to being nervous and becoming fatigued. He said I would get so frustrated that I hit the pool stick on a basement pole or a piece of firewood. He said that he chuckled a little bit inside and thought to himself, *Yep, there's the competitive side of Teddy.* He also said that he felt bad for me because he knew how hard I was trying and how difficult it was for me. He said that he could tell by the look on my face on how frustrated I got when I couldn't give the color and number.

We eventually called it a day and went upstairs. We had a small chat and shook hands, and then Dan had left. We often talk about that visit now as a funny little episode we can laugh at. Overall it went very well.

I had two more visits like this with others before the snow melted. My friends Scott and Dick would pick me up for drives during this time. I would sometimes go to their homes to visit them in their surroundings. When spring and summer came around, I was more secure about walking outside and moving around more. The baseball and softball season were ready to start, and this brought up a few more opportunities for me to get out. After the season started, my friend Gary asked me a few times if I wanted to go to a game and watch with him. I turned him down several times because I was too scared to do this and wasn't ready for that yet, but after a few weeks, I agreed to ride along. This was the team I had played with for many years already, and the same guys I was playing with the weekend I had my accident. This was our softball team, called the Phonies because we were sponsored by the Rib Lake Telephone Company. My buddy Gary brought me to one of our games, which was being played at a small town called Chelsea. He explained to me how we would do this ahead of time so that I had no surprises and was comfortable.

When we got out of the car, we walked together to where the rest of the guys were. As I walked behind the backstop and headed to the dugout area, I could see some of the guys look over to me. I sat up on the bleachers a little ways from where the guys were at. Gary came up to me after their warm-up and told me that he reminded the guys not to overwhelm me with questions or to crowd me. He also said not to worry about remembering any of them; they understood and were happy to simply have me there. As the game went on, each of the guys came up to me one at a time and introduced himself to me. I would say hi in return. No one crowded me or bombarded me with questions. One of the umpires in the game even walked over and said hi. Other than being a little scared and nervous, it went okay. After the game was over, they hung around the dugout area having a couple of beers and sodas. They talked among themselves, allowing me to sit and listen.

This was the way I was reintroduced to my friends in a group atmosphere. The same thing happened with my baseball team, my dart team, and other groups. This process was repeated many times before I was comfortable enough to approach any of them on my own. I always needed to have someone with me when doing these kinds of things. Overall, to some degree it probably took a couple of years of doing it this way. However, I stayed completely away from groups or crowds of people at any given time. I was getting comfortable with one-on-one time, but I could not adjust to group settings. One of the challenges I had with groups, even when it came to my own family, was that I was not able to comprehend and adjust to multiple conversations going on at one time. This would make me anxious. Trying to process more than one thing going on around me was something I had not been able to adapt to yet. My informational intake was so slow that my mind could not keep up if more than one thing at a time was going on around me.

My very first baseball game I went to was with my friends Dick and Teri Iverson. It was a game in Wausau, which is about an hour or so from Rib Lake. While Dick was playing, Teri and I sat off to the side to watch the game. I was beginning to venture out a little more to these kinds of events, though I always needed to have some with me for social support. I didn't want to sit near anyone where I would feel challenged. I could go to a local baseball game or softball game, but I wouldn't go anywhere near the bleacher, dugout, or concession areas. I would either sit in my car and watch it from afar, or I'd take a chair, sit behind the outfield fence, and watch the game. Dick and Teri would often sit out there with their dog, so I sat with them.

It took me up to about six years to overcome this fear. To this day, I still have that fear, but I am able to disguise it in various ways. Even though I had returned to work at one point, I didn't have the capability to overcome my issues with groups, crowds, or gatherings. As I will explain later, my work was more or less one-on-one situations, which I learned to handle better. One thing that I feel the need to comment on is that from the very beginning, my family worked closely on advice from my doctors, and they involved all those around me in a way that let me control my own pace through all this. It didn't hinder or reverse any progress I had made from a recovery stand point. The support system I had helped make these small, incremental advances more achievable. Over time, these were accomplished with various degrees of success. It was never easy and took a lot of mental preparedness, though I would have to self-practice each time I went through with one of these attempts. One of the techniques I would eventually learn to do is role play these events out in my mind over and over again about how I would see things unfolding. I had to do this with everything I did. Without the right support structure, much of this would not have been possible. I know that I have made this kind of statement many times throughout my story, but when you think of each stage of recovery I went through, I would not have been able to do any of this without any of them. Everyone was so supportive, understanding, and patient. Bottom line is they were awesome.

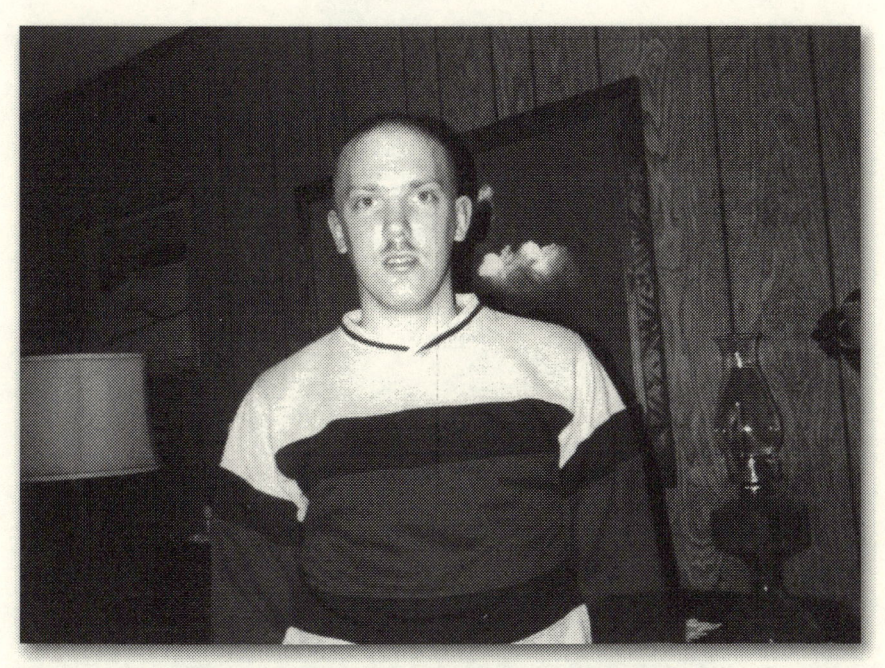

This was taken my first week at my parents
home after my December discharge

Receiving an award from Benny at a Regional meeting

**District Sales Managers meeting –
I am on the far right**

My brothers; starting in the back row –
Conrad, Rodney, Randy, Ted

Zoei and I doing some relaxing time together

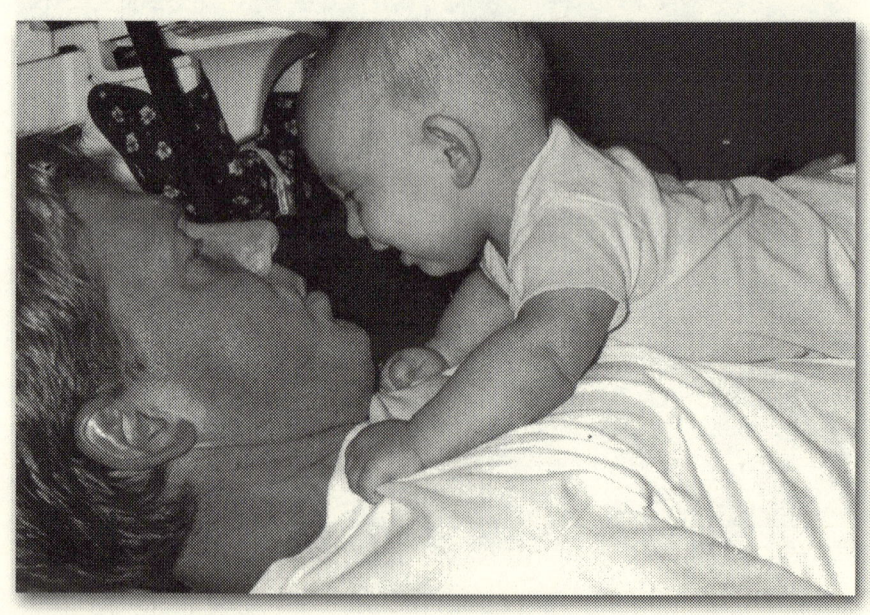

Zoei saying "Hi Dad"

Zoei a little older learning to roller skate

Zoei and I leaving church after a Christmas service

Greenville, S.C. hospital where Kylee was born

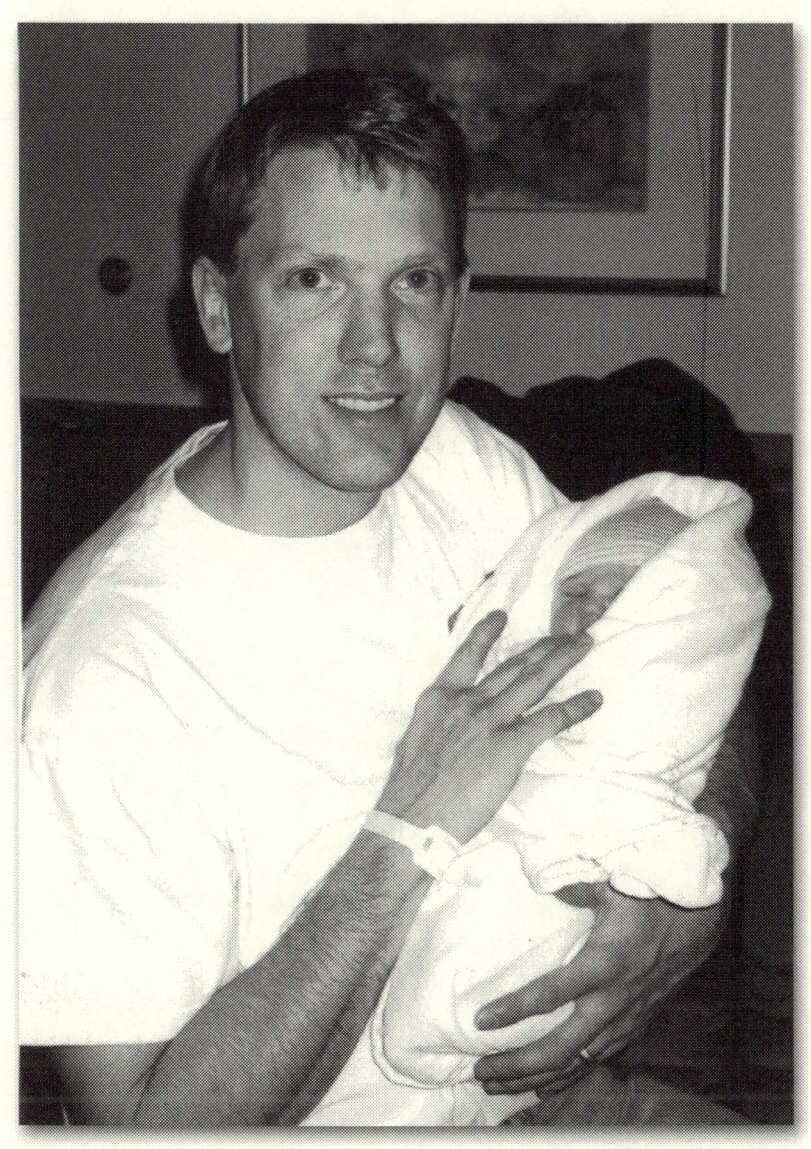

Holding Kylee for the first time

Zoei meeting her brand new little baby sister

Kylee in Kindergarten on Dr. Seuss Day

Kylee working on an art picture

The girls picking out their very first ever pumpkins together

Chapter 15

My Career: Reality or Fairytale?

After nearly two years of disability recovery, things were proceeding well enough for me that I thought I was ready to attempt a return back to work for the company I was with when I'd had my injury. I at least was thinking of the idea, not knowing whether it was too soon. At the beginning of my recovery, the company, through my district manager and others, reassured me and my parents that my job and position would be there for me whenever I was ready to come back. That took so much pressure off me, and it let me focus all my concentration and efforts on medical, physical, psychological, and cognitive recovery. It was the type of work I was doing with Combined Insurance Company that enabled me to attempt this. If it were any other type of work, I don't believe I could have done it. This part of the story pretty much begins when I met Bob Benson, or Benny. After a year or so, when I had been cleared to drive again, I was able to drive myself to Marshfield when I had follow-up appointments. I kept things simple and close to home when driving most of the time.

It was late in 1991 when I received a phone call from someone who worked with Combined Insurance Company. He introduced himself as Bob Benson and explained that he was the regional manager for northern Wisconsin. He said that he had been with the company for many years and was aware of what had happened to me. He was taking over northern Wisconsin, and he was very interested in meeting me. I wasn't 100 percent sure about this because I didn't want to feel pressured and forced into this yet, though I and my neuropsychologist had been tinkering with the idea. He explained that he was staying at the Malibu Inn at Medford and wanted to simply meet me and get acquainted. Medford is about twenty minutes from my parents, so we set up a time to meet. I was a little nervous about meeting this Benson guy.

When we met, we introduced ourselves to each other, and as they say, the rest is history. We had a very casual meeting about me and where things were at. He told me a lot about himself and how he came from Minnesota to Wisconsin to take over this region. Our divisional manager and VP had filled him in on everything that had happened and the promise they'd made to me. His main goal for our meeting was to meet me, introduce himself, and reaffirm that the promise that was made to me would be honored. Bob said that there was no rush, and he wanted me to know everything would work out when the time was ready. He also explained to me that he had reviewed my performance history with the company before my accident, and he was very impressed about where my career was heading and all that I had accomplished in such a short period of time. He said that he would personally do everything that he could to help get me there again, regardless of the time it took. I shared my thoughts with Mr. Benson. I was so grateful for what the company was doing for me, and it meant the world to me and my family. I explained to him that it was a goal of mine to be able to return to work in some capacity, once again support myself, become more independent, and earn a respectful living. I said that I wanted to move away from having to depend on others so much. Even though realistically I knew that I was always going to need some form of support for the rest of my life, it was important to me to have some independence in my life. I am a guy with a lot of pride, and asking for help was never easy for me. Up until now, I'd had no choice, and I wanted to change that. This meeting went smoothly, and I was comfortable with Mr. Benson. It was as though we'd known each other for years and clicked from the beginning. He gave me his number and wanted me to keep in touch with him as things progressed for me. We talked for a bit more, he said that I could call him Benny, and then we parted.

During this time period, I was still doing my home-assigned speech, physical, and occupational therapy. I had a routine with workbooks and activities for each one. These were planned through the neuropsychology department at the Marshfield Clinic, even though nearly two years had gone by. I did keep in touch with Benny, and we struck a chord with one another and eventually became good friends over a short period of time. During one of our phone conversations, I was telling him about the things I was working on at home. He was always interested in what I was doing and wanted to know if there was anything he could help me with. He asked me a question that I didn't quite understand at first. He and I had already discussed different possible scenarios upon my coming back. He asked me when I had my next appointment with my neuropsychologist in Marshfield, and he asked if I wouldn't mind if he had an opportunity to talk with him. Benny said we could set it up in the form of a conference call, where the three of us could speak to each other. I would be with my doctor and conference in Benny. Benny said that this was only a suggestion for an idea he had, and he would do this if I was comfortable with it and if my doctor agreed. I was okay with that, so I talked to my doctor, and he was in agreement, so we did it together from his office.

The three of us discussed things. We went through the introductions and much got right to it. Benny said I had described the kind of therapy work which I was doing at home, and he had an idea that could benefit me greatly. The doctor was all ears. Benny went on to explain on how part of my job was administrative with regards to tracking individual and team sales results within the district; this was done through what was referred to as a manager's black book. It was how managers kept track of premium flow, new sales, manpower acquisition, and route month control. It sounded like a lot, but it wasn't too bad once one knew how to use it. Benny's question to my doctor was whether it be too much of a burden on me if Benny sent to me some of these spreadsheets and worked them into his therapy homework. He also suggested working on route month breakdown of premium. Benny explained that this would fit into what I was doing already because it dealt with numbers, planning, and control, targeting the cognitive functioning part of the brain. Benny felt this would help me advance in decision making and could also help upgrade my informational intake abilities. This could help me reengage myself in more detailed goal setting. It would also give me a head start in those work activities to help me make the transition back to work when that time would come. This would also get me to stretch a little bit more. Benny said that he would send me some sales material, which included sales presentation tips, company responses, and things that would generally be taught through our company's sales school training. My doctor thought it was a great idea because it would focus on what is called executive multitasking. I liked the idea too. I could also stay working on my regular activities as well. Benny said there would be no deadline or pressure from him to complete these tasks. I was to work at my own pace, when I was up to it. It sounded great in theory, but time would tell.

We started this within two weeks and continued doing it for several months, at which time I got the hang of it. Benny worked closely with me on nearly a daily basis so that I would not get overwhelmed or frustrated and stop doing it. Much of it would be by phone, and then in person when he was nearby. Benny and I became closer friends during this period. I felt that he genuinely had my best interests in mind, and he went out of his way to make sure I was working on this at my own pace, no matter how fast or slow I was going. To make a long story somewhat shorter, Benny eventually became my mentor. We had multiple conversations with my doctor, and Benny became very involved with some of my medical issues and personal challenges. I shared most of my medical things with Benny from my doctor. I felt that the more Benny knew, the better he could guide me and understand me. This was something that I could not share with anyone else—not my parents, my brothers, or any of my friends. It had nothing negative to do with what anyone had done for me to this point; it was like their roles in this were completed and successful. It is now up to Benny and me to engage in this head-on.

When I had explained in the first part of my story how I felt God had all the right people in the right places for me at the right time, I had mentioned that he later introduced a new person into my life, and that this person also eventually became a lifeline for me outside of my medical circle. This person was Benny Benson. I had an extremely difficult time connecting with others who were my friends, which included my family. They were aware of this because of my not remembering them or being unable to connect with them. It was easier for me to communicate and interact with someone I didn't know. I didn't have to try to remember who they were, how I knew them, what we did together, or what to say to them so that I wouldn't sound weird. I was able to do this kind of interaction on a one-on-one basis with Benny. Something was telling me inside that I could completely trust this man with anything and everything that revolved around my life, my situation, and my challenges, whether medically, personally, or professionally. It's hard to describe this, but I had this strong gut feeling, and I felt it in my heart as well. As all this unfolded, I still had unconditional support and help from my parents and others in the way they had since the beginning of my recovery. However, the possibility of me trying to reenter the work arena was something they could not really help me with.

One main concern we had was that if I tried to return to work before I was truly ready, it could backfire and halt my progress. The overwhelming pressure to support myself and take on too much too soon could halt what I was trying to do. The implementation of this had to be at the correct time. My neuropsychologist was always in the loop with what Benny and I were doing or trying to accomplish. We got input from him on everything so that he was there to step in from a medical standpoint if he noticed something going wrong from his end of things. Again, none of this was in any way easy for me, but the one thing that I am absolutely sure of is that if I did not have Benny there with me, I wouldn't have been able to do this.

Chapter 16

Reality Check: A Tough Learning Experience

During the time Benny was working closely with me, he called me one evening and asked me if I had tried grocery shopping yet. I said that I hadn't, because I had a tremendous fear of entering a public place without the backup of having someone with me. I was terrified that I would run into someone who knew me, and that person would come up and start talking to me. I had huge anxieties about this because I would have all these mental gymnastics of who this person is and how they knew me. It was the same old story that has plagued me from the beginning. Until I was able to come up with a "one size fits all" response to someone I knew, I shied away from engaging every time. Benny was aware of my fear of going into a store, bank, or post office by myself. Even though the hospital had those mock scenarios at the rehabilitation center, I had not tried it in real life.

Benny asked me if I knew how to do it, and I said no. He laughed a little and said something like, "Buddy, how do you expect to eat when you are out on your own again?" He knew that one of my goals was to overcome this huge block I had on myself when it came to entering a store or public place without fear. Benny asked if I had made out a grocery list, and I said no. Through my therapies, one of the things I relearned to do was how to use a phone book, look up a name, and find the number. When I initially worked on this, I did not know that the phone book was set up in alphabetical order. I did work on making out a grocery list at one time, which was then used to walk through the mock grocery store they had on the unit. Other than that, I hadn't done either task since being discharged. He asked me if I remembered how to do it. I said not really. Benny walked me through how to make out a grocery list and explained how to go about doing it. He said that if there was something I needed, I should write it down on a piece of paper. If there was something else that I needed, I could write it down on that same piece of paper until I had a small list. This would be easier for me than sitting down and trying to think of things I needed. It seemed simple enough, but this was new territory for me.

We made out a very short list over the phone, nothing complicated or confusing—or so it seemed. I think we had just five or six items on the list: a candy bar, a gallon of milk, a toothbrush, toothpaste, and a box of cereal. One would think, "How hard could that be?" Benny explained on how to go in and look for the items by looking at the aisle signs hanging from the ceiling. I was able to read them, and the whole idea was to do it without asking anyone for help to find these items on my own. He knew I was scared to death to do this, but he took the time to walk me through it a couple of times. I told him that I would try to do this within the next day or two. One thing that I never did with any of my doctors or with Benny was lie to them. They were sincerely trying to help with all of these things, and if they suggested something for me to do, I would promise them that I would try really hard to do it. I felt that it would have been easy for me to just say yes, claiming I did it and it was okay, but it would not be of any benefit to me getting over that particular hurdle.

When I was prepared to attempt this, I would rehearse it in my mind over and over and over again. I would try to visualize it in my mind until I felt mentally prepared to do this. Sometimes it would take me up to half an hour to go through this with other things I attempted to do. This trip to the store took me a little longer. It was about twenty minutes to the grocery store in Medford, and I was still rehearsing it in my mind. When I arrived at the store and turned off my car in the parking lot, I froze and started to feel my heart pound faster. I turned the radio on to distract me. I then started to rehearse in my mind what Benny had instructed me to do. I think it took me another half hour to get the courage to walk in. I forgot to mention that I had also called my neuropsychologist and explained to him that I was going to attempt this, and that Benny had walked me through the process. In the parking lot, I was sweating, nervous, and panicky. From the way I was feeling, one would think

I was about to rob the darn store, but I was simply there to get a candy bar, a gallon of milk, a toothbrush, toothpaste, and a box of cereal. Benny and I look back on it now and laugh about the whole thing, but I sure wasn't laughing about it then.

I walked into the store and started to look for the aisle signs, as he told me to do. The first few weren't what I was looking for, so I walked along the end of the aisles. Then I came across a sign titled "bathroom" or something like that, and I found the area for the toothpaste and toothbrush. I stood there and stared. I couldn't believe all the different varieties of toothpaste! The first thing I thought of was that Benny never told me how many different brands there were or what kind to get. It was the same thing with the toothbrush. I started to get nervous. I picked one out and looked at it. Then I picked another one and looked at that one. Which one should I get? I put both of those back and picked out another one, and then another one. I didn't know which one to get. I would say to myself, "Come on, Ted. It's only toothpaste, for crying out loud. Just figure it out." There were too many to look at and choose from. The trouble I was having was that my brain wasn't able to take in all the information of different names, brands, tube sizes, and colors of the packaging. I cognitively could not compartmentalize the thought process of taking in the information and holding it long enough to compare it to another brand and size. It would roll around in my mind and get mixed up. I couldn't process it and come to a conclusion. I didn't know whether I should buy based on the tube size of the toothpaste, the brand name, or the packaging color. I didn't understand the ingredients or how to figure out the purpose of each brand. I was trying to think of a way to get out of the store without looking like an idiot. I started to choke up because I couldn't do this. Then I thought if people were watching me, they would think I was odd.

After standing in the aisle for nearly twenty minutes pretending to read a tube of toothpaste, I set it back on the shelf and walked out. I didn't look for any of the other items. I went straight to my car, put my head on the steering wheel, and cried. I felt very stupid, foolish, and humiliated. I ended up driving home, sick to my stomach about how it went. I didn't tell my parents about it when they got home from work. I called Benny later on, and the first thing he said was, "Hey, Teddy Goodrich, how'd the shopping go today?" I said that it didn't go very well and explained. He laughed a little bit and said, "Hey, that's all right. Nothing ventured, noting gained." Benny wasn't laughing at me, but with me, to lighten my mood. I started to chuckle a little bit after talking to him. He said it was a good thing I didn't start out in the cereal aisle or the candy bar section, or else I'd probably still be there! He said simply walking in there by myself was a big step. We went through the entire experience. Doing this little exercise made me realize one thing, and that was to set small daily goals and objectives, as I did with my rehabilitation. Now I had to adjust those small goals to the reality of daily living activities.

The next day I called my neuropsychologist and went through the whole process with him. He was excited for me as well and said congratulations. I said I had a simple task to do and fell well short of it—I'd failed miserably. He asked what made me think that I had failed. I repeated to him again what had happened. He obviously knew I was upset about how it turned out, and he said, "Let's step through this one step at a time." He asked me what my objective was. I said that it was to go to the store and pick up the items on my grocery list, but I didn't get them, not even one. He said, "That's correct, you didn't get them. But what did you learn by not getting your items?" I said I didn't know, and he broke it down for me. He said, "First you made a list of things for you to get. Have you ever made a grocery list out before, no matter how long it was?" I said that I hadn't, other than in therapy months ago. He said that was a goal set and achieved. He knew that I was able to get to the grocery store. He then asked me how long it took for me to enter the building. I said it was close to thirty minutes. He asked me if I had ever done that on my own before, and I said I hadn't. He said that was a goal set and achieved. He then asked me how I was able to find the shelving where the toothpaste was. I said that I had walked along the end of the aisles and looked up at the signs, as Benny told me to do, till I found the aisle I was looking for. He said, "Right. That is a goal set and achieved." He then asked me if I physically picked any toothpaste off of the shelf and looked at it. I said I did. He said that also was an overall objective I had set and achieved. I said that didn't matter because I hadn't come out with anything. He said that didn't matter. He explained to me that by setting that one objective, I had accomplished several goals that I have never done before. How could I not call that a success?

This reminded me of how Benny explained it. I described to my doctor how Benny showed me how I should implement this into all my activities. When I go out into the field to relearn my job, I would be setting a weekly objective, with daily goals to support the success or failure of that objective. He said that it was like reaching for the moon and coming back with a handful of stars. The doctor reminded me how I'd used goals to heal and recover from my injury over the past two years. He then explained that I needed to redirect that same goal-setting process into my daily activities, especially now I was getting ready to try to reenter the workforce. When I look back on this now, it really was a unique way to give me the perspective I would need to prepare me for the next step. He said, "It's not always about whether you fail or not, but it's how you got to that point. Life will always give you rejection, just as your career will. It's about going through the steps and doing it the right way. By doing it the right way, it will put you in position to succeed or fail." He said this was all he or anyone would ever ask of me, and he had a strong feeling that Benny would tell me something similar. He asked me to put my trust in Benny and let him guide me along using my strengths, not my weaknesses. He said with each small advance, I would reach where I wanted to be, just as I had in the past.

Chapter 17

A Career-Making Decision: Do It Now

My doctor and I had been discussing off and on that it was getting close for me to give working a try, especially after he had seen how Benny was working with me. It was probably a little earlier than I should have tried, but through this process of working with Benny and the things he was introducing to me as homework assignments, he had me prepared as best I could be under current circumstances. Even if I would have waited till a later date to do this, I still had all my medical issues to deal with because none of that was going to just go away. I decided to take the plunge to set this in motion.

Before we would hire someone to fill a sales rep position, we would first do an initial interview with them. If at the end of that interview the person was interested in the position, we would set up what was called a field demo. This was where the person would go out with a sales manager or district manager for an afternoon or a full day, to watch and observe what we did on a daily basis. This way the interviewee could see what we do and whether he or she could see doing it as a career. We would try to have the interviewee see what we called the good, the bad, and the ugly. In other words, they would see how we service and renew establishing policyholders, review their current coverage, handle claim situations, and add updated coverage or additional family members. The other part we would show them was how to get referrals from our established business, which we called a warm lead, as well as making cold calls. That simply meant calling on a business, a home, or a farm to ask if they would be interested in taking a look at something that could benefit them and their families. The last part we wanted them to witness was the rejection that would obviously go along with any type of sales. Not everyone wakes up in the morning to buy insurance. But most important, we wanted to give the interviewees an opportunity to see the income he or she could make in this position, so they knew that they could earn a decent living. A properly planned field demo would see an average of up to four hundred dollars earned within that day, which was very conceivable by working the system as it was designed.

My first step was to go out and be field demoed for a week or two, to observe and learn. My district had a new district manager by the name of Ray Albaugh. Ray and I had worked together since I was originally hired, so he knew me well, and this was why Benny had asked him to do this. Ray and his wife visited me often in the hospital, and he knew most of what I had gone through, so he was very patient with me/ We had a connection while working together. One of the things we worked around was that I had to take periodic breaks during the day due to fatigue. I couldn't go a full day without some rest due to my sleep deprivation, which was one of the residual effects from my brain injury. Ray and I did more reconnecting during these two weeks than we did in sales. The idea was to get me more familiar with our system and sales material than it was to produce results; that would come later. Benny talked to Ray and me every day to see how things were progressing. I had never let my insurance license lapse during the time I was off, because I kept up with the bi-annual renewal while I was recovering. I did not do any sales-related activities during these two weeks; I simply followed Ray's lead and observed. I did engage in conversations with our clients when the opportunity was there.

After the two weeks were up, Ray felt that I was more than ready, and I agreed. The following week I sat down with Benny, and we talked about a game plan. He had reviewed and inspected my level of knowledge on what I had learned so far. He was confident that I was ready for phase two: sales school. He wanted to send me back to sales school for one week to polish up on my material, learn when to use proper responses, work on my sales presentation, and brush up on the product knowledge. Remember that I was way ahead of the game at this point because of the material Benny had introduced into my home therapy assignments months ago. I was scared to death and yet very excited to jump back in.

When I arrived in sales school and proceeded with the training, it did feel somewhat familiar to me. This was one of two sales schools within our six-state division. One was in Chicago near the corporate office, and the one I was attending was in Minneapolis. During the week I was there, I had the opportunity to meet new people and make some new friends, some of which I would be seeing later on in our region. There were maybe twenty people in all. Over half of them were from neighboring states. One could just imagine the fear I had whenever it was my turn to demonstrate sales scenarios. I still had a very difficult time relating to people, especially within groups, but it was different when I was around people I didn't know. I didn't have to concentrate and focus on past memory issues to remember who, what, where, and when. I was there for a specific reason, and I was being given a track to run on. I had to meet certain requirements though in order for me to graduate from sales school. The trainers there felt that I was well prepared after the first week of a normal two-week course. If I wasn't, then they would have suggested I stay the second week. Sometimes people needed to extend their training there for an additional week if they were struggling with the training. Benny kept in touch with me throughout the week, and he met with me the following week. We reviewed the sales school week and discussed what was going to happen next. He said that he was going to have my district manager, Ray Albaugh, field train me the following week. Shortly after I was originally hired, our district had merged with another district to our north. This merge took our district size from two counties to five. This was how Ray and I became acquainted.

Benny gave me two homework assignments to do the rest of the week and that weekend. I should think of the goals I wanted to achieve, and I should simply relax. He said that Ray was going to have everything laid out and ready for Monday. Ray was a good man and a very good trainer. I said that I really wanted to shoot for a PAL Award next week. Before Benny and I parted, I thanked him for everything he had done for me. It meant a lot to me that he took such a personal interest in helping me get to this point. He said, "Teddy, you did all the work. I was just your guide and was along for the ride. You deserve all the credit for the hard work you put into this." It may be true that I got myself here, but I was also well aware that none of this would have been possible if Benny hadn't taken me under his wing and spent an ungodly amount of time with me.

IN MY OWN WORDS

Benny called me Sunday evening, the night before I was officially back as part of region again. He asked me if I had done the two homework assignments. I said yes. I'd written down my overall objective and the goals to help me get there, and I tried to relaxed as much as I could. I wanted to achieve a PAL Award as I had once before, but Benny said to let the results be whatever they turned out to be. He said the results would come. My field training week was to focus on product knowledge, know-how and when to implement it, and working the system to get me into the right field activities.

I also said that I had four specific long-term goals that I wanted to accomplish. Goal number one was to properly engage in working the system as it was designed, and I could achieve these goals only by doing this. Goal number two was to work my way to writing twenty policies in a day. Goal number three was to write fifty policies within a work week, and goal number four was to write one hundred policies in a week. This last one was known as a winner's score and was the standard of excellence for managers in field performance. Benny was proud of these four strong goals that I had set, and he said he believed these goals seemed well thought out. He knew how tough this was going to be for me, but he knew the work ethic I had and said that he felt that I had not overreached on the goals. I said that the only thing I didn't have were any dates by which to have these goals completed. He said that they were believable, very conceivable, and definitely achievable. He went on to say that it did not matter how long it took to reach these goals, or how many breaks in a day I needed to take, or whether I put in a half day or a full day. He said that I had already proved to him how hard I worked at things, and that he wasn't worried about that. He said, "I'm here for you, Ray is there for you, and you drive this at you own speed." Wow, did that take a ton of pressure off my shoulders! I teared up from joy and gratitude.

Benny also had some other good news for me. He told me that I wouldn't have to worry about my income. He reinstated me to my manager's contract and put me on a four-hundred-dollar weekly pay guarantee. If I were to make more than that during a work week, that was what I'd earn. If I earned less than that, I had the safety net of four hundred dollars each week. By being reinstated to my manager's contract, I was going to receive overrides on everyone in the district. That would add an additional three to four hundred a week on top of what I made in the field on my own. He was also going to remove all the usual requirements a sales manager had to do to fulfill the duties of that position.

He said that all he wanted me to do was focus on what Ray was going to teach me, and the rest would fall in place.

I said, "Benny, I can't thank you enough. I can't believe this is happening." I again teared up with gratitude and excitement.

He wished me luck and said he would be talking with me each night this week. He said, "Welcome back, Teddy. Relax and have fun."

When I met Ray on Monday morning, he had everything in place for us. Most of the prep work we did to begin a work week was done Sunday evening. I had already gone through this process with Benny months earlier, but Ray had it completed already. I had told Ray what Benny had done for me, and he said congratulations. Ray shared with me that he already knew that Benny was going to tell me this sometime before we started our work week. Ray told me that I deserved this, and now it was time to roll up our sleeves.

I want to make a comment here before I continue. When you think of everything that Combined Insurance has done for me, you can plainly see the kind of company I was working for. This process also demonstrated the type of people who were there to help me get to this point, making this transition as smooth and easy as possible. In all my time since, I have never seen a company work with an individual as this company has done with me. The following is a summary of my first week in the field on my own. Our regional office was located in Eau Claire, and Benny's regional assistant would send out weekly good news bulletins and newsletters to share good news within the region and rank the reps' and managers' results. She would also include any achieved awards, recognitions, or advancements that were made. This is how the good news bulletin went out.

> Welcome back to the NOW Region and the Combined World, Ted Goodrich! We're glad to have you back after 20 months of disability.
>
> Last week, April 13th–18, was Ted's first week back in the field on his own since his accident so long ago. Ted had a great week, with 20 Giants (aka policies), 20 Amendments (aka disability income policies), 1 SHIP (aka sickness hospital indemnity policy) and $770.63 in income! Ted was working in Browning township, a rural area outside of Medford, WI. Because Ted was out of the field for so long, he wanted to do all the right things: he did not want to develop

any bad habits—no "road patrol." Ted decided to put the pressure on the system, and not on himself, and to maintain PMA. Ted was patient, pleasantly persistent and used tools he learned at Sales School. First he worked the system systematically (at a pace he could tolerate), and secondly he used a lot of humor in his voice.

Ted Goodrich has a great adversity—greater than what the average person has to deal with. Ted had to start all over; he had to learn how to walk, talk, and think. But for Ted, this was an opportunity to put into his head only positive things. From the very beginning Ted employed the PMA philosophy, using it every day in the hospital and throughout his rehabilitation. He set daily goals (such as learning to tie his shoes) and he kept his mind on only his daily goals. Ted's experience helped during his first week back in the field. His daily goal was to drive into every driveway—and if he got a talk in, so much the better. At one point, Ted found himself passing the driveway to a farm. "I passed the driveway, went down to the corner, turned around, thought a few minutes and went back. I showed the policy, was patient, had to come back at a later time, and sold 8 giants and 3 amendments," Ted says. "All the Combined knowledge—the talk, rebuttals, etc.—wouldn't help a bit if I didn't work Essential #7." Ted says you must learn the proper activities in the field—you can't learn that in school. Ted gives much credit to Ray Albaugh, who field trained him and showed him how the system works. It took away a lot of the anxiety Ted had.

For the future, Ted's goals are to constantly be in the right activities while selling the whole roll, and to eventually work himself up to a Winner's Score. Ted, you already are a winner in our hearts! Welcome back!

The first week for me went better than I could have imagined. All the months leading up to this moment was worth it. It felt wonderful to do this on my own. My parents were ecstatic, and my brothers were so excited for me, as were others. I also talked with my doctor throughout the week so that he could assist me in anxiety management and other methods I could use to keep me grounded. It wasn't easy, and I did have a lot of anxieties popping up all over the place, but I was able to calm myself and get relaxed before each contact I made. I was sure that I went into every call professionally with a casual demeanor, a smile on my face, and confidence.

When Benny and I reviewed the week, we broke it down and went through what went well and what didn't go so well. I could have done things differently at times or been better at other times, but overall I was successful in all aspects of our business. I renewed and met with our established policyholders, I had also worked our system that put me in the position to make cold calls and warm calls (also referred to as leads), and I got in several presentations, just as I did with this young farm owner. It was the husband whom I had presented this to, and he liked the policy, the benefits, and the cost. He asked me if I could come back later in the day to show this to his wife, because it was something they would decide on together. I said that would work out fine and asked what time was best for them. He said sometime before chores and milking had to be started. I stopped back at the time he designated. His wife also liked what I was showing her, and she liked how the coverage would benefit them, especially with the kind of work they did on the farm. They were also reassured by the fact that so many of their neighbors and people they knew carried a policy like the one I was showing them, because he and his wife had never seen this before. This was an awesome start for me, and it made a nice income as well.

Chapter 18

Goals Made, Set, and Delivered

In this chapter I will share with you a few different things. It will include goals successfully achieved both on a personal level and a career level. They are intertwined with one another, but I'm going to try to separate them to a certain extent. First I will begin where I left off with the previous chapter.

I had a very positive work week in my first week back in the field on my own. I had four specific goals which Benny and I were going to work on together from here on out. There was no time limit on accomplishing these, but we tried to plan them accordingly as I became stronger in the field and in a geographical work location that best fit my goal. For example, my first goal was to consistently work the system on a daily basis, and I could do this in my own district and home area. My work activities became consistent, but I worked this around my energy level and at a pace I could tolerate. My second goal was to write twenty policies in a day. To achieve this, I would have to work in an area where I had the opportunity to give twenty full policy presentations per day in a controlled environment. Based on the ratio of non-sales presentations compared to sold presentations, that meant I would need to see enough new potential opportunities or policy holders get five nos to each yes, on average.

The two things that I worked very hard on were field activities and referrals. I did not have the energy level to perform a full day of sales activities, and I sometimes needed up to three breaks to get through a work day. For years I have battled chronic fatigue due to severe sleep deprivation. I have had this since my accident, because it was part of the damage I had to my brain. Sometimes I would go through two or three nights with no sleep. The longest stretch I had gone with no sleep was seventeen days. This was always one of my challenges. Benny and I had a plan in place that would allow me to work on my strengths when working in my home district. Then when the company had what were called incentive weeks, I would go on the road to another district and spend the week with Benny, and he would be with me to work on my weaknesses or areas where I needed to improve. Regional incentive programs were training and sales oriented programs. It usually consisted of the top twelve sales reps and mangers coming together for a week to work toward a common new sales goal. These were also to give a boost to a district that may have been behind schedule or lacking in productivity. It was also a great way for salespeople to achieve award advancements. There were company incentives that could be won on a daily basis and for one's total week results. Some of the incentive programs that were done regionally and nationally were sweethearts week, presidents week, challenge week, and founders week. There were generally national or regional incentive programs scheduled for each month of the year. I have been on plenty of these programs, which helped me advance when I started with the company. Benny would include me in these programs, but not as my usual role as a district sales manager. Most of the guys and gals on these programs were people I'd grown into the company with, and they were very excited about having me back as part of the team. Benny would usually hold me back after the morning kickoff meeting during these weeks and go through my assignment with me. I would arrive Sunday evening along with everyone else and plan out everything. Benny would share with me a little bit about the area, the history of the township I was working, and what the possible potential was. Whenever I went on the road with him, he would do his best to keep me working close to the hotel. That way if I had to stop early for the day or needed to take a break, I could drive back and rest at the hotel, as opposed to resting in my car.

After a few months of working this system, I was eventually able to target my daily peak periods when it came to field productivity. As I progressed in my administrative abilities, I began to check in the sales reps I had reporting to me and keep track of their sales results and income. This was part of the paperwork Benny had me doing early on. I always did the very best I could on everything. Some weeks I did well, and some were very frustrating.

I was also in regular contact with my neuropsychologist through all this, usually an average of two times per month. Some contacts were by phone, and some were office visits.

It took me nearly one year to reach my second goal of writing twenty policies in a work day. It was in February 1993 that I accomplished the feat. I was making new sales each week, whether it was a new face sale or adding an additional family member and working leads. My work was small but successful. I did have new cold call sales as well, but nothing was consistent yet in that area. Benny and I continued to work the same strategy we had been doing. I wouldn't go on all of these programs with him, but I would go when I felt ready and as I was getting stronger in the field. My confidence level was also becoming more consistent, and my sales and income were more consistent.

I proceeded in the same manner as I had over the past year or so since coming back. There were many times when I had major anxiety and issues with fatigue, but it never got to the point to where I wanted to give up or quit. Benny would talk me through it and allow me to take a few days off when those challenges arose. I don't know of another company that would work with someone as they worked with me. Benny was my regional manager, and he never once got upset with me or frustrated with my results. Neither did the management above him. My policyholder retention was one of the highest in the region at 97 percent. That meant that I didn't need to write a lot of new business to run an increase in my designated areas of work. It took me about another year to reach and achieve my third goal, which was to write fifty policies in a work week. I had achieved this goal in October 1993. It was also an award called an Eagle Award. The requirements of this award were to sell 50 policies in a week and earn over five hundred dollars. I have made higher income than this in a week since I had returned, but not together with fifty policies in a week. I was beginning to manage my work time very well with my peak performance periods. In other words, I was beginning to learn how to work smarter and not harder. Achieving this third goal was a huge weight off my chest.

My fourth and final goal was to write a winner's score, which was one hundred new sales polices in one work week. That can be a very difficult task, and that is why it is considered a standard of excellence of the company, from a production of performance standpoint. Not everyone can do this. When I started with Combined Insurance back in October 1988, I had achieved all requirements within eight months or so. It has taken me close to two years to reach half of this. Benny and I planned and worked on my fourth goal on many occasions, and I had always come up short. Sometimes I fell miserably short. But on those occasions, I always gained success in some other form. Keeping my mind positive while going after this last goal was very tiring and wore on me both physically and mentally. Benny kept me positive and in the right frame of mind.

To fast forward things a little bit, the company was introducing a new program called Worldwide Impact Week. We knew of this program about six months in advance. The regional managers were given plenty of time to condition and prepare their regions for this major program. As we neared this date, Benny already had plans in place from a regional standpoint. He had the area already picked out and the team of managers the wanted on this program. The entire region was involved in this, but the team of twelve was the region's top performers. Benny wanted me to be on this program and had personally picked the area which he thought was the best opportunity for me to achieve my fourth and final goal. He got my assignment to me about two weeks in advance so that I could properly break it down in a way to get me off to a fast start, instead of giving it Sunday evening when we arrived at the hotel. This would help start my mental preparedness for this program and my goals for the week. After I had broken my assigned area down into daily objectives, Benny and I talked about this program whenever we talked. This kept me focused on the program, the environment of the program, and the national attention it was going to get. There were also going to be some very nice incentives to win with this. It was going to be a very challenging week for everyone participating, and I was starting to feel that pressure building within me. The time for me to go all out and do this was now. I had the right environment and the perfect area to work, from what Benny had discussed with me. I also had the support of the top twelve writers in our region. I knew each of them, and I knew they would help keep me to my game plan.

We arrived Sunday evening to kick this off. There was a lot of excitement, and the conference room was done up with large charts on the walls to track everyone's results. I started to feel very intimidated once I walked in and saw everything, yet I was excited to be part of it. The people who were there were great, and I knew they were rooting for me because they knew that I was going for my winner's score this week. After our Sunday evening kickoff and conditioning for the week, we were able to head to our rooms or hang out, talking to each other for a little while. I chose to hang out with some of the guys for a little bit, and I had a soda and a bite to eat, which the company had catered. I talked with Benny for a while and then returned to my room for the night. I looked over my assignment for about a half hour to learn policyholder names, the area, and whether any claims were pending that I would need to address.

Morning seemed to come early, and I didn't get much sleep that night. We all met at 8:00 a.m. to officially kick off the week and give our daily and weekly objectives. As I roamed the room with my eyes, I noticed my name was written on the wall tracking chart, and I got a big lump in my throat, thinking, *This is it. It's all or nothing this week.* When it came time for Benny to go down the list of names on the chart, each manager gave a weekly goal and then a daily objective. After each one was done, a round of applause filled the room, more so than other programs I have attended. Mostly it was due to the fact that everyone was charged up for this national program, and we were in competition with another region from a neighboring state. When it came to my name, Benny yelled out, "Teddy Goodrich, welcome to Worldwide Impact Week, buddy." The applause from the guys exploded. Everyone stood up while clapping, hooting, and hollering. This was even before I'd even given my objectives! When I said that I was going to try to write my first one hundred-call week since my return back to work, they applauded again. I started to choke up when I gave my weekly goal and my daily objective. It felt awesome to be part of that again. Before I'd had my accident, I had written many hundred-call weeks. I had been back to work now for nearly four years, and I hadn't come close to writing one, though everyone knew I was working really hard to accomplish this.

After we were done with that, everyone left to hit the field and get a fast start. Benny came up to me and said, "Relax, work your plan, and have fun. Take the pressure off yourself and put it on the system. This is your time to shine and let it all out." He wished me luck and said that if I needed anything, I should give him a call. I headed out for the day. I was working the township and town of Eau Galle. I had nearly five thousand dollars in policyholder premiums to renew there, so it was time to set this thing in motion.

When I got to my starting area, I took a few moments to gather my thoughts and get myself in the right mind-set. As my district manager once told me, it was time to roll up my sleeves and go right at it. We usually worked late on these programs because we didn't know when the best time was to see the policyholders we needed to see due to their work schedules. I planned my breaks around morning, midday, and early evening. The day started off kind of slow for me as I got familiar with the area, however, it picked up about midday. I had renewed about one thousand dollars in premium and had eight new polices by 1:00 p.m. I took my afternoon break and ate a packed lunch I had put together. I had a few things lined up later in the afternoon, which included some callbacks. A callback was when I gave a full presentation and then asked to come back to show a spouse. I went on one of my callbacks about 5:30 in the evening. On that call, I had closed a twelve-for-one, which was twelve policies at one household. When I walked out of the house, while walking to my car, *I thought, Wow. I am already at twenty for the day, and it's only six o'clock.* It took me nearly a year to write twenty in a day, and here I was, already at that point. I was excited as heck.

    I stopped by two renewals and got a referral from one of them. They gave me the name, address, and time to catch a friend at home. They said that he worked in the woods as a logger, and he knew of the company and the kind of coverage this was. They said the best time to get hold of him was between 8:30 and 9:00 p.m. I was getting tired, and it was still two hours before this guy would be home. I felt like heading back to the hotel because I was already at twenty for the day, which was the pace I would need to write one hundred by Friday. I decided to make a few more calls so that I could later follow up on this lead. I renewed one more established policyholder, and then I came upon someone working in his garage. I decided to stop by and see him. He was a younger guy, and I was able to give him a presentation. He bought from me, and I left with four more. I was now at twenty-four sales for the day! I was excited now, and I was so tempted to call Benny and share my good news with him. All I was thinking about was going back to the hotel to share this in our good news part of the evening. I had one more call to make, and that was the logger at 8:30. I was tired and thought that I would stop in about a half an hour early. Luckily, he was actually home. I approached him, introduced myself, and said that his friend had asked me to stop and show my policy to him. We went into his house, and I showed it to him. I sold six policies between him and his son. I was now up to thirty policies and over three hundred dollars in income for the day!

I was on cloud nine on my drive back to the hotel. When I got back to the hotel, I put my work stuff in my room before going down to the conference room area. The first thing I did when I walked down there was look for Benny. When we made eye contact, I gave him a big smile, and then I looked up to the tracking chart. Everyone had reported in except for two people. There were four people with twenty calls and one with twenty-four. Benny could tell that I'd had a good day by my expression, and he enthusiastically said, "Teddy Goodrich, how did it go for you today?" I told him that I had a thirty day, and he and the guys cheered that good news. I again choked up and had to hold back some tears. The other two guys came in, and I was the leader of the day. The next closest guy to me was at twenty-four. There was food catered in and drinks for us, so nobody had to go out to find a place to eat. I made a plate up, grabbed a soda, and went back to my room. I was wiped out from the day, there was too much going on in the conference area, and I had a hard time focusing on keeping up with things. Benny said I could tell him about my day tomorrow.

In the morning, everyone wanted to get off to a fast start again, so we shared our good news and then gave our daily objectives. Some of the guys had daily objectives of writing thirty, and others wanted to write twenty. My objective for the day was to write twenty, in order to stay on track. I have never started a week off like this, and I didn't want to waste it. After the meeting, Benny asked how I'd slept last night, and he said I should stay relaxed and work my day just like I did yesterday. I said, "Wish me luck," and headed out.

It was about a twenty-minute drive to my work area. I again broke the day into three parts by planning my breaks as I did yesterday. The day started out better than the previous one. My first break was schedule for about eleven o'clock. I made five presentations by my first break. Out of those five, I sold four policies. By the time my second break had come around, it was three o'clock. I had written another eight policies, which put me at twelve for the day. I was getting nervous as the day went on because I had never been in the situation before, but I was also excited. I had lunch during my second break and rested for about forty-five minutes. I then worked some premium to catch up on that part for the next hour or two. Then I forced myself to work leads and make cold calls till I went back to the hotel. I was now at twelve and was close to my daily objective of twenty. During the two hours between seven and nine o'clock, I looked for farmers and loggers. As I got more into my area,

I became familiar with the people and the kind of work most of them did. I ended up giving two more sales presentations during that two-hour block and sold four-for-one on both of them. When 8:30 p.m. came around, I was sitting with twenty policies for the day, which put me at fifty in two days. My heart was beating so fast that I had to take some deep breaths. When I got back to the hotel, I put my work things in my room again and went down to the conference room. The first thing I did was look at Benny and then the results board. Four guys were not in yet out of twelve. Benny asked me if I had any good news from the day; he knew I had some because I was smiling and trying to hold it in. Some of the guys who were already in turned and looked at me as I said I'd had twenty. The guys were so happy for me and gave me high fives.

Benny put my results up on the board, turned to me, and gave me a smile and a thumbs-up. He knew I was tired, and so he didn't ask me much about it because he was waiting for the rest of the guys to report. I once again made a plate, grabbed a soda, and went back to my room. I was so nervous about it that I didn't know what to say, anyway. I had earned nearly another three hundred dollars that day. I was very close to having my premium done as well. Things were working well for me out there. I stayed in the right activities and worked the system as best as I could. It became a numbers game.

On Wednesday morning, we went through the same daily kickoff with our objectives. Mine was another twenty. I wanted to stay consistent, keep my plan unchanged, and not get overconfident. Benny had me stay back for a bit and again asked me if I got any sleep last night. He told me to take a deep breath and not change a thing. I should go out and have fun because I was leading everyone on the program. He wanted me to keep focused and not to let anything distract me or affect my attitude. He wished me good luck, and I headed out. All I was thinking about on the way to my assignment was finishing my policyholder renewals and getting twenty in as quickly as I could. I was sitting at fifty for the week.

I had given seven sales presentations that Wednesday, and I sold five out of those seven. At the stops I sold sixteen-for-1, a twelve-for-one, and three eight-for-ones. That brought me to a daily total of fifty-two policies. Talk about a fantastic week so far!

Never in my wildest dreams did I believe the week was going to unfold for me as it had. I drove back to the hotel at about 7:30 p.m. and was the last one in this time. I was nervous but still excited. This time one of the other guys yelled out, "How did things go for you today, Teddy?" When I told them that I had fifty-two, they nearly fell over.

Benny got quiet, looked right at me, and said, "Are you serious?" He shook my hand, gave me a hug, and said that he could not be happier or prouder. The group clapped, whistled, and rang some cowbells that we had in the room. Some of the guys asked me how I was doing it and getting multiple family sales. It wasn't that I was suddenly better than they were, but they wanted to know what was working for me, and they wanted to hear me share my good news.

I had finally accomplished my fourth and final goal, so all was good for me. I did the usual and went back to my room with a soda and a plate of food. Benny came down to my room a little bit later to congratulate me. He said that all my hard worked paid off this week, and he couldn't be prouder of me for finishing my goal and leading from the front on this program. He asked me, "Did you know that you are the first person in the NOW region to write a winner's score in 1995?" I said I didn't know that. He said that was including sales reps and all managers. I told him that I was 80 percent done with my assignment, and it looked like I would have it completely done by Saturday. He asked me if I could do him a favor. "Are you up to field training one of the sales reps tomorrow, Thursday?" I said that I could do that, but I didn't know how much I had in me. He said, "Just do what you can, and spend some quality time with him."

The next day I took out the rep, and we worked in his assigned work area, which was about fifteen minutes from mine. We had a successful day together by coming in with sixteen. One thing I always did on a field training day was all of the production, sales, and income we made went to the sales rep. As a sales manager, I never split or kept any of the production we did together. Some managers liked to split income for the day, but this was a rule I decided to make regardless who I went out with. If a sales rep is struggling, the last thing he needed is to have his field trainer take half of the day's production and income.

The entire week for me was more than I could have expected. During the week I also learned a lot from other managers regarding different sales techniques, responses, and presentation styles. I also saw how difficult it was for some to finish their one hundred calls. This helped make it clear to me that this was a tough thing to do, and it no longer mattered to me that it took me this long to finish my final goal. The company was also taking national calls at the corporate headquarters in Chicago. The president of the company was personally taking calls from all winner's score writers. I had my opportunity to call him from the conference room that Wednesday night. I was congratulated and told that I was one of the top managers in the country by finishing my winner's score by Wednesday night. It was only a ten-minute call, but it was very cool. Combined Insurance Company was a Fortune 500 company, so this was a pretty special thing.

Benny asked me if I was doing okay, health wise. He didn't want me to overdo it considering my objective was already in. Benny knew that I was working really hard at this, putting in some long hours and pushing myself. I said that I was okay and would go out to finish up my area, follow up on some leads, and make some cold calls. He said I should take a slower pace to finish out the week and enjoy my success.

Some of the guys had to push it hard up till the end on Saturday in order to get in their winner's score. I finished the week strong, selling another twenty on Friday and two on Saturday morning. All the preparation that Benny and I had done leading up to this week had paid off big time. My weekly grand total was 130 policies sold and an earned income of $1,077. I called my parents and my brothers Saturday night when I got home, and they were very happy for me. I also called my doctor Monday and shared the good news with him. He was overjoyed by the good news. I hadn't called them till the program was over, just in case I once again failed on this final goal of mine. Benny's regional sales assistant had put together a special good news bulletin for the program to share all the good news that went on within the region for Worldwide Impact Week and the results of the program Benny was running during that week. The following was the lead story in the news letter.

> Impact 100 Writer:
> Ted Goodrich
>
> Very possibly, Ted Goodrich had the greatest impact on the NOW region during the week of January 9–14, 1995. By coming in Monday night with a lead from the front, a 30 day, Ted actually caused the other players to kick it in gear. Ted continued his leadership role throughout the week, finishing his 100 calls by Wednesday and selling another 30 Giants besides! This is a fantastic end to a story that began over 2 1/2 years ago. Ted was a sales manager at the time

he incurred a very serious head injury that could have taken his life. After months in the hospital and months of therapy and recovery, Ted felt he was ready to try the field again. At the time, Ted set 4 specific goals for himself. They were to (1) work the system, (2) write a 20 day, (3) write 50 Giants in a week, and (4) write a winner's score. Ted has now accomplished all that he set out to do!

During last week's 100 call, Ted made the following impact: He was the first sales rep in the NOW region to write a 100 call in 1995. He was the second in the Midwest division, and he was number 23 in North America! Ted also broke many personal records with last week's 100 call.

New Record	Old Record
52 day	50 day
3-day 100 call	5-day 100 call
130 Giants/week	108 Giants/week

1st ever Golden Grover Award
100 + $1000!

During my career with Combined Insurance, I had written a winner's score on only two other occasions. The first time was the following year during Worldwide Impact II, 1996. The second time was when I had field trained a new sales rep coming out of sales school to a Gold PAL Award in 1998. I still was very successful in my career and accomplished many good things.

However, during this period of time, many changes were taking place. Benny left Northern Wisconsin to accept the position as regional manager for Northern Minnesota. He was originally from northern Minnesota, as was his wife. When this opportunity became available to him, he made the move back. Benny did not leave me hanging in the wind; he and I stayed close friends all this time. He was still my mentor when it came to helping me with any of my medical, personal, social, and work challenges. As I had mentioned earlier, he is the only person I completely trusted outside of my medical circle. We talked constantly and would see each other whenever possible.

My tenure with Combined Insurance would eventually come to an end after nearly twelve years. The reason I left was because there was a major change ready to take place in my own life as well. I was going to become a dad, and I was really excited about that. I didn't want to travel each month and work the long evenings; that was starting to wear on me physically. I also wanted to be home every night to help take care of the baby and not be a part-time dad. I didn't want to miss out on anything. Over the years, I have seen many moms and dads working with Combined Insurance miss so many events and occasions with their children due to being on the road and working in other districts, all of which were essential to advancement. However, I always promised myself that if I ever had to make the choice between my career (with late work nights and being away from home for two weeks or a month) or my family, I would choose my family. After nearly twelve years with Combined Insurance Company, I decided to leave. It was October 2000, and it was approximately eight months prior to our first child being born. I talked this over with my wife, Benny, and my doctor before doing this. It was a tough decision, yet an easy one.

Chapter 19

Sadness Looms Once Again

When I left Combined Insurance, I had already made the decision about a month prior to leaving. I had talked this over with my current regional manager, and he understood why I was making the decision. I had reached out to a friend of mine who was working at a central Wisconsin radio station. I have known her for nearly six years because I had worked with her husband for six years when I was with Combined Insurance. I explained to her that I was making the change and looking for something new, and I wondered if she knew of any possible openings in the sales field. I explained that I would need to find something that kept me in a sales-related position because it was one of the few types of work that would allow me to manage my days and work around my health status. She said that there was a very good chance that a position could become available where she was working, and it would be a perfect fit for me. It was a position to work a specific area, and it could possibly allow me to continue to work out of my home office, which I had done with Combined Insurance for all those years. This was a crucial factor in any possible career change to help me with longevity and being successful in my activities. A position did in fact open up with this radio station, and I went through the interview process and was eventually hired. I began this new career change in October 2000. The timing of this worked out beautifully for me. When I gave my two weeks' notice to Combined Insurance, I had this all set up, which made it possible for me to make the change with no downtime in between. I eventually went on to work in radio broadcast sales for about eight years, at which time things went bad; I will touch on that a little bit later.

As a family, we had to face another one of life's unexpected turns that happened five months before the birth of our first child. It was the unexpected death of my older brother, Conrad. Conrad was just one year older than me and was the first of four boys. He was also named after our biological dad. Our dad had passed away when I was thirteen and Conrad was fourteen. Going back a little bit, in 1990 when my accident occurred, Conrad was the person standing next to me in one of the pictures while I was in a coma. If you recall, I had tried to answer the one question I had for myself: Why would God allow me to survive the injury I endured and leave me here like this? I believed the reason was that God had a plan for me, and he knew of something in my future which he wanted me to experience or be a part of. I also said that it would take me years to figure out what that could be. Well, I now know what those experiences were to be. One of those reasons was to fall in love, because I had met my wife about six years after my accident. I met my wife in early 1995 at the place of business where I did my banking as I was now handling my own finances. Our first contact with one another was when I had driven up to the drive thru window where she was working as a teller. I didn't know how long she may have been working there, but this was the first I have seen her. She caught my eye right away. She primarily worked at the home office branch of the bank which is located in Medford. I had moved out on my own by this time and lived in a two bedroom apartment in Rib Lake, which by the way had a branch office for the same bank. Whenever I had banking business to do, I would generally go to our branch in town. After I had met her, I found myself driving to Medford to do my banking which was about twenty minutes away. Over the next few months we really seemed to enjoy talking to one another when we interacted. I would think to myself; *This girl really likes me.* After about three months I finally got up the courage to ask her out on a date. She said yes. As usual I had spoken with Benny on several occasions and told him all about her as this was new territory for me. It was mostly to settle my anxiousness and worries about what she would think about me and my history. She agreed to a second date, and then another and the rest seem to fall into place. When the time came for me to share my health history with her, she was nothing but very positive and supportive of all that I went through. As our relationship grew, so did her confidence in me and in my abilities. She was supportive in my job, my ongoing recovery activities and the goals I had set in place for myself. Within a year we had gotten engaged and set a wedding date for the following year. I wasn't trying to meet someone, nor was I actively searching. I believe it was all part of God's plan for me. I also believe he wanted me to witness and experience the birth of a new life coming into the world as part of my family—after witnessing the loss of another life. The event ended up being the death of my older brother Conrad.

Conrad was coping with what is now known as bipolar. He wasn't dealing with it so much when I had my injury, but over the years things were happening with him that no one could identify. He was going through various tests, and his doctors were unable to nail down what was going on with him. Over time, he was diagnosed with bipolar. With the diagnosis of this medical condition, it made some specific treatments available to him that hadn't been there for him in the past, most of which were apparently working. While I was recovering from my brain injury, he was slowly deteriorating from this disease. I wasn't fully aware of it because I had all of my own issues going on. My parents and brothers were aware of it, and once again my mom and dad were having to deal with something tragic that involved one of their children. When things started to get really hard for him, I was working in radio broadcast sales. He was aware that he was going to be an uncle because our first baby was due to be born in July 2001. He himself had two little girls at the time, aged ten and thirteen. He was a single dad and did not see his girls as much as he would have liked, which hurt him very much. Those little girls were his life. Conrad was a very family-oriented man. There wasn't one thing that he wouldn't do for people if they needed help, even if there was some cost to him in one way or another. I know this can be said of anyone who dies unexpectedly, and I'm not saying this as a cliché: he really was one of those good guys whom you would like to know and have in your life. He was a hardworking and all around nice guy.

While I was working in radio sales, part of the area in which I had to work was the Rhinelander, Tomahawk, and Minocqua areas, also known as the Wisconsin north woods. I had been staying with him at his apartment on Thursday nights in Rhinelander for a couple of months now. This was so that on Fridays I could finish up on leads and follow-up appointments. I would work up in the area early in the week and then stop in to see him and confirm that I was coming up on that Thursday. I had stopped in to see him on a Tuesday the last week of February. I popped in as usual to see that everything was all set. As I was leaving his apartment, he kept holding me up by starting a new conversation. I didn't think anything of it, and we would finish talking about whatever it was we were talking about. Then when I started to leave again, he would start up another conversation on a different topic. I thought to myself, *Gee, someone has a lot to talk about today.*

But then he started to say things like, "Ted, you know you are welcome here any time, right?" I said yes and added that I appreciated him letting me stay with him, because it saved me a two-hour drive on each Thursday and Friday. He said, "You know that you're welcome to come in and make yourself at home, even if I wasn't here." I said yep, and I knew where the key was. I thought that he was referring to him out running an errand or something. I ended up saying to him that I really had to go, and I would see him Thursday at about four o'clock. That was when I would end my day to do my reports and plan for the next day. My work week ended up being changed on Wednesday. I was to work at the radio station all day Thursday and was to have one of the senior salespeople train me on radio ad scheduling. I wasn't going to be driving up north that day, and I hadn't called him to let him know about the change in plans.

The day was moving along fine when the receptionist came up to me and said that I had a phone call; it was my mom. I didn't think anything of it until I heard her say, "Teddy, this is Mom." After hearing the tone in her voice, I got a bad feeling in the pit of my stomach.

I said, "Mom, what's wrong?" She said that Conrad's lady friend had just called, and something had happened to Conrad. I asked what had happened. My mom said that Conrad had died. I replied, "Oh, my God, no. What happened?" My mom said that she didn't have all the details and that he was taken to the Rhinelander Medical Center. She said that they were heading up there, and she asked if I could meet them there. She and Dad were waiting for Randy and Rodney.

When I hung up the phone, I almost collapsed and started shaking. The person training me that day happened to be the same person who'd helped me get hired. I told her what my mom had just told me and said I had to get to Rhinelander. My friend said; "Teddy, we'll go right now. I'll drive you." We left immediately without saying a word to anyone. She called our general manager back at the radio station from her phone while we were driving up there, and she explained to him what had happened.

It took us about forty-five minutes to get there, and we seemed to be ahead of my parents. I had all sorts of things running through my mind and was very glad that my friend offered to drive me. Conrad's lady friend was outside of the emergency room when we arrived at the medical center. When I got out of the car and went up to her, she looked at me and said that he was gone. I asked her, "Do you know this for sure?" She said that he was dead. I said, "Oh, my God. Are Mom and Dad here yet?" She said that she'd just talked to them, and they were about twenty minutes out. We hugged each other for a few minutes, crying.

I asked her what had happened. What she told me was way beyond my ability to comprehend, and I wasn't prepared for it. I was thinking it was an accident or something to do with this heart, because he was having some heart trouble as well. She said that she went up to his apartment to invite him downstairs for supper. When she entered his apartment, she said that she found him hanging in the doorway. She said that she ran to him to lift him up but couldn't. She tried to find a knife, scissors, or anything to cut him down, but she couldn't find anything. That was when she noticed notice what he had used.

Conrad used a type of thick wiring cable, and there was nothing she would have found to cut through that. She called 911 and continued to try to lift him enough to take pressure off of his neck. Conrad was a big guy, and she just couldn't do it. I felt so bad for her, having to be the one to find him like that. I asked her if she would be okay if I left her alone. She said that she would be okay and was going to wait outside for Mom, Dad, and my two brothers. I wanted to see him and asked if she knew where he was. She softly said he was in the morgue.

I walked over to my friend to share with her what had happened. She gave me a hug and said, "Teddy, I am so sorry." She said that she would stay there with me for as long as I needed her. She was aware of my past history and thought that I may need a little extra support in dealing with this. I was grateful to her for that. I hadn't called my wife yet because I wanted to be 100 percent sure. Also, she was pregnant, and I didn't want to have her at home alone and stressed by such news.

I went in alone to find the morgue area. There were a couple of nurses in the hallway who took me to where he was. I was so nervous that I didn't know whether I should go in, but I took a deep breath and went inside. When I saw him lying there, I nearly threw up. I didn't want to believe this was happening.

I stood there looking with a blank stare. I walked over to him and grabbed his hand. He was so cold already. I started to cry. I leaned closer, gave him a hug, and kissed his forehead. I looked at him and said, "Con, you dumbass, what the hell was so bad that you had to do something like this?" I really didn't mean what I said, but I was so mad right then. I kissed him on his forehead again and said, "You idiot. You stupid idiot." I cried and ended up sitting in a chair next to him.

Mom, Dad, and my brothers came in about ten minutes later. When they came into the room, I stood up from the chair. I couldn't help but see the look on my mom's face. I didn't say anything; I didn't know what to say to her. My dad and brothers were in shock, and they started crying when they saw him and said nothing as well. My mom walked over to him and set her head on his chest, just under his chin. Then she gave him a hug and kissed him on his cheek. She stood there next to him, stroking his hair and holding his hand, not saying a word. My mom looked at me with her eyes filled with tears, and she gave me an awkward smile. It was hard for me to look into her eyes. My dad and brothers did not crowd her and stayed back while she was with Conrad.

A little time passed when my mom said, "Con, just so you know this, I love you very much, and I do understand why you did this. I think we all do." After a few moments, my mom walked over to me, gave me a long hug, and said, "Thank you for being here for him so that he didn't have be in here alone."

I said, "Mom, I am so, so sorry. I got here as quickly as I could." It hit me at that moment: this was why God wanted me to survive my accident. He knew this day was coming for Conrad. I believe he knew that my brother was struggling with this, and it was going to come to an end for him one day. I also now believe that he wanted me to survive so that my parents, especially my mom, wouldn't have to mourn the loss of two of her four sons.

It was after that point I was going to call and tell my wife what had happened. I said to my friend, "Thank you for driving me up. that I will be okay now." She left for home.

When calling my wife about the news of this, I didn't want her to be alone when I called her, so I first called our friends Dick and Teri Iverson and told them what happened. I asked if Teri could go over to the house and be with my wife when I called her. I feared any complications with her pregnancy if she got overstressed. Maybe I was overthinking it, but I didn't want to take the chance. The Iversons lived only six miles from our home, and Teri was kind enough to go over right away. It was reassuring for me that my wife had someone there when I made that call.

I look back and sometimes think that Conrad had two little girls in his life, so why would God take him and not me? At the time of my accident, I was younger, alone, and had no children. I don't know if this is the right way to think of it, but the entire chain of events leads me to believe this. One thing that I do take some comfort in knowing is that I was the last one to see him alive on that Tuesday. The downside of knowing that is wondering whether there was something that I should have picked up on that he said, to tell me that something was wrong. But that is something anyone in a similar situation asks himself. I tried not to think of that.

A few days later, when we were cleaning out his apartment, we made two startling discoveries. The first one was that he had stopped taking his medication. We found a large plastic back under his mattress that looked like months' worth of medication. Why he stopped taking his medication, we will never know. The second discovery was a cassette tape marked "Last will and testament." On this tape he described in great length why he was doing this. He also had addressed a message for each of us, including his daughters. However, those are private details which I will not disclose.

There are a couple ways that we as a family could try to absorb such a tragedy. The first was that Conrad had to be in such a distraught stage of his life that he felt he had no way out other than to do this. Second, he didn't have any intention of hurting someone else. When something like this happens, many times you will hear that another life is taken as well. We thank God that he had no intent of this. Another way to look at this was that he was in so much pain that he no longer wanted to live with the way things were for him. We know that he is now at piece and in heaven with God and our dad. However, that was no comfort to his two small children, who now had to live the rest of their lives without their dad.

Sharing this news with them was so very sad and was not something anyone wanted to do. We had gone over to their home with their mother and told her what had happened. It was their mom who shared this news with them. When his lady friend found him on that Thursday afternoon, the door frame which he used in his apartment was very, very low. The cable he used was cut just long enough that if he would have changed his mind at the last minute, all he would've had to do was stand up. He kept his legs bent so that his knees were only inches from the floor. This tells us as a family that there was nothing any of us could have done to prevent this. He had made up his mind. I often think to myself that if I wouldn't have had that change in my work week, would I have been the one to find him? Or would I have been there early enough to interfere and stop him from doing this? Only God knows the answer to that question. As with the loss of any loved one, we think of him often, we love him, and we miss him dearly. It's been fourteen years, and it still saddens our hearts. However, one of the greatest joys that I could have ever possibly experienced was soon to happen, and that was the birth of my first child.

Chapter 20

Here Come The Rainbows

The birth of our new baby was kind of like a rainbow, knowing and seeing something beautiful was going to bring a little joy back into our hearts. With a new baby about to be here, one of the things that I always had in the back of my mind was, how would I be as a dad? This was mostly due to the things that had happened to me, and I wondered whether I would be able to adjust to this kind of change. This was a planned pregnancy, so I was prepared for it and was ready for this new chapter, but it was still a thought I had in the back of my mind. This may be most common with any new parent about to go through the birth of a child and raising a newborn, but I was especially worried about it because of my inability to adjust to my surroundings and to sudden changes. So what did I do? I did what I always did with any new change that happened in my life since my injury: I talked through this change with my doctor and with Benny.

When all was said and done, they both reassured me of my abilities, and they believed that I would be a great dad. I had to stay with my support structure and go through this process as I had done with everything. I also had the reassurance of my wife that I would be a great dad. Even though I was worried, I knew that I would be fine; I simply needed some reassurance.

When the time of delivery had arrived, it was an anxious moment for everyone. They gave me the choice of being in the delivery room or being in the waiting area. I chose to be in the delivery room. I wanted to be a part of the birth of our baby, and to be there in support for my wife. Also, I was the breathing coach. All of the worries and concerns I had were washed away when I heard that soft little cry and then the words, "You are the proud parents of a baby girl."

Throughout the pregnancy, we did not want to know the gender ahead of time. As long as he or she was born healthy, it didn't matter to us whether it was a boy or a girl. The new mom was the first to hold our brand-new little girl, and the joy of her overwhelmed the both of us. There were lots of tears of joy going on at that moment. We had a name picked out ahead of time. We now had a new member of our family, Zoei Marie Goodrich, and she was the most beautiful, precious baby girl that God could have ever given us.

When it was time for me to hold her, my wife had handed her over to me, saying, "Zoie Maire, how would you like to meet your dad?" Words cannot describe the feelings I had at that moment.

I held her firmly because I didn't want to drop her, and I gave her a little kiss on the forehead. I said, "Hello, baby Zoei. I'm your dad." I touched her little nose, her little chin, and her tiny fingers. I turned to my wife and said, "Can you believe that we are actually parents now?" I'm sure that many new parents feel this same joy of bringing a new life into the world, but for me it seemed so different. I believe it had much to do with what I had gone though in my life up to this moment. I said to this bundle of joy that I was holding in my arms, "Zoei Marie Goodrich, I will love you and be the best dad I can be, and I will always be there for you." I kissed her little fingers and gently passed her back to my wife. Watching them begin that mother-daughter bond was so cool to see.

Everything went very well over the next day or two, and then mom and daughter were discharged to go home. A whole new world began for our little family. Over the next few weeks and months, things went as expected. The only challenge that came about at one point was trying to get Zoei to fall asleep by herself at night. She seemed to have a hard time of doing this, as many babies do. We had tried some of the usual techniques, which included soft music, a CD with various sounds, and the running of a vacuum cleaner. We tried several other methods, but none of them seemed to work.

The last thing we tried, which was explained to us by the delivery doctor, was setting down Zoei in her crib, walking out of the room, and letting her cry herself to sleep. Her doctor said that this was a tough thing for parents to do, and it would take a few days of this to get Zoei to adapt to this. They thought she was colicky and had a hard time falling asleep. We had tried this for one or two nights, and it was a tough thing to do. It was very heart-wrenching to me for one simple reason. Zoei's crying took me back in time to where it made me reflect back to the time when I was in the hospital so many years ago. Right or wrong, this was what immediately popped into my head. When I went into Zoei's room when she was crying, it was as though she was asking for someone to help her. I immediately thought of the night when I was crying and screaming for someone to help me, for someone to look down at me and see that I was awake and asking them to not let me die. It broke my heart to let Zoei have that same helpless feeling. Even though it was two totally different situations, I still felt that I had to help her. I knew nothing bad was going to happen; I just had this need to let her know that I was there for her and it would be okay. I had to pick her up and comfort her. I would hold her close to me and talk to her. "It's okay, sweetheart. Daddy's got you." I found myself walking her until she fell asleep, at which time I would lay her down, and she slept through the night. The next night we tried to let her cry herself to sleep again, and it was the same result. I would go in, pick her up, and walk her until she fell asleep. This happened for quite some time. When I wasn't walking her to sleep, I would either rock with her in the rocking chair or sit on the recliner with her until she fell asleep. Sometimes we would lay down on the sofa, and she would fall asleep on my chest. I myself still couldn't sleep at night because of residual effects I had from my brain injury, so it was no toll on me to do this. We believed that this could be harmful in some way, producing an improper sleep cycle for Zoei. This was a justifiable concern we had, and her delivery doctor shared similar thoughts, but she also said that my doing this was not hurting Zoei.

Some nights seemed better than others, but I walked or held Zoei every night until she fell asleep for nearly one year. Yes, you read that correctly—one full year. She did eventually grow out of it and was able to sleep on her own. She may have been able to do it sooner, but it became a routine more for me than it was for her. It was maybe not the correct thing to do, but nothing else seemed to work, and if this was what it took, then this was what I needed to do.

Two years quickly passed, and we got the news that we were expecting our second child. This was a very exciting time for us. Zoei was going to have a baby brother or sister. Again, we didn't want to know the gender. As long as he or she was born healthy, that was the main thing. However this delivery was not going to happen under normal circumstances. The timing and the place of delivery didn't go as planned. It was once again one of life's unexpected turns that had to be dealt with. We needed to pack our bags and head out for a little cross-country drive. A few days before the baby's due date, we had received some sad news that lead us on our journey to central South Carolina. It was a tough decision to make, and we would rather have not made the trip, but it was one we had to do. We were hoping that we could make the trip there and back before the delivery. Of course it didn't quite work out that way. My wife wasn't able to fly, so driving was our only viable choice.

What we feared eventually happened. The baby wasn't going to wait till we got back to Wisconsin. My wife went into labor about an hour from our destination. Fortunately for us, and by the grace of God, a hospital was within ten minutes of where we were at, and we made it there with time to spare. The newest member of the Goodrich family was born in Greenville, South Carolina. It was not what we had planned, but God was watching over us, and things turned out as well as could be expected. Zoei had a baby sister.

As before, we had a couple of names picked out ahead of time. Zoei's little sister was born in a Southern state, so there was a little change in plans again. The names we had picked out didn't seem to quite fit her. When my wife held her and looked at her for the first time, she said, "This little girl looks like a Kylee ... a Kylee Rose." That is how her name came to be Kylee Rose Goodrich, which added a slight Southern touch compared to the other names we'd had in mind. Zoei was now two years old and was excited about having a baby sister. She was very excited to hold her. When I was holding Kylee for the first time, I knelt down to so Zoei could see her. Zoei leaned in and gave her a gentle kiss on her forehead. It was a cute, priceless moment.

Here's a funny little side note: We were a small traveling family from Wisconsin and ended up having a baby in Greenville, South Carolina. Believe it not, four out of the six nurses that we got to know while we were there were die-hard Green Bay Packers fans! They adored our quarterback, Brett Favre.

Whoever have imagined anything like this? That was pretty cool and gave Kylee a little bit of a Wisconsin connection after all. The delivery and everything went very well, which allowed us to be there for the circumstances that had brought us so far from home. Both mom and daughter were given the thumbs-up for discharge two days later. Now we had a long drive home ahead of us. This was a little worrisome, and we were going to have another new adventure ahead of us. Traveling home with a new baby halfway across the country—yikes!

The trip went better than expected. It took a day or two longer to get home, but it went well for the most part. For one, Kylee slept nearly the entire way, other than when it was her feeding time. We also made multiple stops along the way during the day so that everyone could stretch. Zoei was a real trooper all the way home. We finally got home safely and we were happy to be back.

Kylee now knows all about her little adventure, and I hope to take her back to Greenville one day so she can visit her birthplace. Both girls are growing up into wonderful young ladies. They both are now in middle school. Kylee is a seventh grader, and Zoei is in eighth grade this year. They have grown up so fast, and both of them are very kind-hearted and respectful girls.

Chapter 21

A Decision to Be Made: Quality of Life

The things I would like to share with you in this chapter will give you a picture of where I am now at in my life. I will also share a few other things that have occurred in the past few years.

I had worked for the radio station I had mentioned for about eight years. I was successful in what I was hired to do, and I have always had above average to excellent performance reviews. In late 2006 I was having some difficulties with my health. I was having increased fatigue from performing physical activities. It wasn't just doing heavy strenuous activities, as I have always had trouble in that area due to my chronic fatigue and sleep deprivation. I am referring to light yard work and lawn mowing. Things didn't seem quite the same with me physically, and I ended up having several doctor appointments over a month or two. Whenever I seemed to reach a level of physical exertion, my body would get very tingly, I would have shortness of breath, and my chest would get tight. I would discontinue what I was doing because I was fearful of the way I felt. I became more concerned with this as it occurred more frequently.

In May 2007 one of my physicians scheduled a stress test for me at the Marshfield Clinic. For those who may not know what a stress test is, it is simply walking on a treadmill. During the test, they would slowly increase the speed and the incline of the treadmill at three- or four-minute intervals. The first three minutes went okay. At the first interval, they quickened the pace a little bit and raised the incline slightly. Two or so more minutes passed, and I was starting to have a hard time keeping up with it. Within a short period of time, I wasn't able to keep pace by walking, as I was supposed to do. It got to the point where I had to jog to stay on the treadmill. It then reached the point where the other technician had to press on my back and push me a little bit to keep me up toward the front of the treadmill, because I was stumbling and nearly falling off. We were only at the second stage and were about seven to eight minutes into it when we had to stop. I was falling off the back end and stumbling far too much. I was heavily gulping for air and felt faint, and my arms and legs felt week and shaky. The test was concluded, and they removed the monitors and said it was okay to put my shirt back on.

They asked me if I was okay. I said I thought so, but I didn't feel quite right. They had brought me some juice and crackers. I started to feel really weird, and what I was feeling didn't seem normal. Prior to this test, whenever I tried to do something with any physical exertion, I had a numbness and a weak shaking feeling go through my body. When we did this test, they asked me to push it a little more than I normally would, because I explained that I would usually quit whatever I was doing when I started to get this feeling.

After I was dressed, about ten minutes passed, and I asked for another glass of juice to drink. They said to take a few more minutes, and they would be back to take me to my doctor's office so he could review the results with me. I had asked for another juice and said that I really felt weak; my legs felt like they were going to give out. They had asked me if I would like a wheelchair to take me back to my doctor's office. I asked for a few more minutes, and the technician went to get a wheelchair for me. As she was coming back, I stepped toward her and had collapsed onto the floor. They called for some help and I was instantly not very responsive. I suddenly couldn't move my arms or my legs, and I didn't know what was happening.

I was lifted onto a gurney and taken to a side room where they started attending to me. My entire body went rigid. Everyone thought that I was having a stroke. It was either that or a heart attack. It happened so fast that when I collapsed, I tried to catch myself with my left arm. I went rigid so quickly that my arm froze, sticking up in the air. When they tried talking to me, I couldn't speak. I was barely able to move my lips, my tongue, or my eyes. All I could feel were tears running down from my eyes into my ears. I was really scared, and they didn't even know what had happened. They quickly ran tests on my heart and lungs, and everything seemed normal. After this was done, they called the emergency room and notified them they were bringing over a patient and gave my symptoms.

I wasn't able to speak to them to tell them what I was feeling, so they did a process of elimination on what could be wrong. They found that my organs had overheated so much to where my body released a massive amount of carbon monoxide into my bloodstream. This caused a sudden change in my body's electrolytes, and it completely froze every muscle in my body, from my eyelids to my toes. Nothing moved.

They remedied this by the use of IV fluids to restore the balance of my electrolytes. It took about five hours before I could start moving my arms and legs, and I was finally able to bring my left arm down to lay it by my side. This is the medical episode I referred to earlier in my story that set off a whirlwind of events. My doctor suggested I take a few days off of work to rest and to get some of my strength back. I had to be careful not to exert myself physically again until some further tests were done. I ended up taking a week off from work and having a couple of follow-up visits to figure this all out. It came down to the fact my body was not able to continue on as it had over the years of moderate to severe sleep deprivation and chronic fatigue. I was not able to get the adequate sleep to allow my body to recharge itself. It was like a battery growing weak in its cranking power, not being able to hold its charge anymore. This episode soon after affected my other residual deficits, which I had worked so hard to overcome. That episode and other outside stressors made it difficult for me to maintain a certain level of cognitive ability. Things started to unravel for me over the next couple of months.

In February 2008 I left the radio station and tried to move my future forward by accepting a position with a local TV station as a salesperson to do television broadcast advertising. I tried hard to do this position for as long as I could. I had some success while at the station during the year and a half that I was there. In early 2009 I needed to request a three-month medical leave to get a handle on these new symptoms before it snowballed on me. By that time it was already too late. During those three months, I had to revisit medication management to help me with issues such as anxiety, chronic fatigue, severe panic attacks, and worsening sleep deprivation. I also had to engage in other treatments that I hadn't had to do for a very long time, which included some brain retraining techniques and cognitive counseling. During this three-month period, all of my physicians from the neuroscience department at the clinic and hospital had discussed and agreed that there was very little they could do for me medically. My physicians included a neurologist, a neuropsychologist, a clinical psychologist, a psychiatrist, and the Department of Sleep Medicine. They all came to the same conclusion. They felt it was time for me to consider the possibility of having to apply for social security disability. I had medically qualified for this over all these years, but I was fortunate enough to find my way back to working and being able to support myself and my family.

During this entire episode, I had Benny there to talk me through things like he had done so many times for me in the past. I had talked extensively about this with each of my physicians, my wife, and Benny. I also talked this over with my parents and family. I did not want to take this avenue I was having to now look at. It was a path I hoped would not come. Maybe that was wishful thinking, considering my overall recovery and the successes I had achieved.

The reality that I had to apply for disability was hard for me to accept. Benny and I had talked about this in great detail. I needed his honest opinion and true thoughts. He has never given me anything less in all the years I have known him. He said that sometimes it's hard to know when to call it quits. He said that I have recovered more than anyone ever imagined, and I went back to work when many would have given up and taken the easy way out. On top of that, I had worked longer than anyone had expected, with a lot of success and achievements. He explained to me that I'd had a choice long ago to take the easy way out, and I chose not to. He said that I wasn't quitting—I had actually accomplished everything I had set out to do. There was nothing more for me to prove. He agreed with my doctors and suggested I follow their advice; they knew my health better than anyone. The longevity of my life span was seriously threatened now, and this wouldn't affect just me anymore. I asked him what people would think of me if I were to do this. He explained to me by saying he doubted anyone who knew me and what I had gone through would ever think that. Second, he said, "You have nothing to be ashamed of. You have a family now, and you have to think about them and the quality of your life. That is all that matters now." It was as if he was a fly on the wall during the meetings I'd had with my doctors.

Benny knew I didn't want to go this way, but I didn't have a choice anymore. I again talked it over with my mom and dad, as well as with my brothers. I also talked this over with my friends Scott and Renee Zondlo, and

Dan Fliehs. They echoed what had already been said to me: no one realistically imagined me getting to where I was today, and they couldn't think of anyone who would think badly of me. I really struggled with this, but I eventually came around and accepted this new reality. My doctors again explained that if I were not to do this, there could be a higher probability of my having a shortened life span, especially with some of the new issues at hand.

When this was repeated again, the first thing I kept thinking of was my family. My daughters, Zoei and Kylee, kept popping into my mind, and the decision became clearer for me to make. I now had to focus on managing my health from a quality of life standpoint. I had to do this. We started to pursue this course. I had to let my employer know that I would not be returning to work at the television station. A whole new phase was put in motion. My employment ended, and the long process of social security disability began. The entire process could take as long as two and a half years.

In the winter of 2010, I had another somewhat traumatic event. It was after a heavy snowfall, and I stopped by my mom's one afternoon. I had called her before I came out, and she said that Dad was out back plowing snow. She had asked if I could maybe shovel some of the snow away from the picture window on the deck. The deck adjoined the house, and it had drifted up onto the large window. I said that I would do that as soon as I got there. It wasn't much to do, just a few feet to clear it away.

Mom said that she looked out the window and saw my car in the driveway, and she figured that I was out back by my dad, because the snow was away from the window. My mom later said that she had left their dog, Lexi, out about a half hour to forty-five minutes after seeing my car. What my mom didn't know when she looked out the window and saw my car was that I was lying on the west side of the deck, unconscious. When she saw my car, she didn't even think of looking in the other direction. I had slipped and tripped backward over a five-foot post. Each fall my parents would put plastic over the deck and lay four-by-four and four-by-six posts on the deck to keep the plastic in place. They would do this to help preserve the deck during the winter season. With the plastic under the snow, it made it very slippery. I had initially slipped on that, and I fell backward, tripping on one of those posts. I had nothing to reach for to break my fall. When I fell, I hit my head on one of the now frozen posts lying on the deck. I struck the back of my head and was knocked out. The next thing I knew, I was awakened by their dog. Lexi had been licking and pushing her nose on my face. This was what brought me to consciousness. This first thing I thought was, *What the heck happened?* I was cold and couldn't move right away. My head hurt, and I tried to get up.

I couldn't move my arms or legs. I yelled for help, but no one heard me. I could hear the tractor running back by the shed where Dad was still plowing snow. After about fifteen minutes or so, I was able to move my arms and legs. I couldn't get up, but I was able to pull myself along and crawl off the deck and into the garage. It took about twenty minutes to do this. I got to the door in the garage and knocked on the door. My mom opened the door and found me lying on the step. She said, "Oh, my God, Teddy, what happened?" She ran to get my dad, and they helped me into the house. I told them what had happened, and they covered me in some blankets while I was lying on the kitchen floor. I said that I was okay but felt like I was going to throw up. They sat me up and called the Marshfield emergency room, which that with my history of head trauma, they should bring me down for an examination. It wasn't so bad that I needed an ambulance, so my parents drove me down right away. A CT and MRI of my head showed bruising on the back side of my brain, but no bleeding or apparent swelling. That was wonderful news, but nonetheless the fall was still harmful to my brain. It was considered to be a severe concussion to mild brain trauma, due to the amount of bruising and the time I was unconscious, which was estimated about a half hour or so. I did not have to stay overnight in the hospital, but I spent some time in the emergency room. Thank God that Mom had let Lexi out, and that the dog came over to me and started licking my face, or who knows what could have happened. I did have some subtle effects, but nothing very serious—just a good scare, I guess.

I had requested the help of a disability advocacy firm in Minnesota. This firm was nationwide, but the office I had contacted covered the tri-state area of Wisconsin, Minnesota, and Iowa. They helped by assigning someone to take care of gathering all the necessary medical information since 1990 and my most recent health condition. She would get all the reports, forms, and applications filed properly because I wasn't able to keep track of all that had to be done.

It was also during this period that my fourteen-year marriage began to dissolve, and it eventually ended. There really are no easy words to describe how or why a marriage ends. What makes it even more difficult is when you have a family where small children are involved. My wife was a home mom from when Zoei was born through both girls entering school. It was a decision we both made and believed to be in the best interest in raising our girls. The changes over the past couple of years however had begun to weigh heavily on our relationship. The changes in my health, and my ability to work was in question; putting a heavy burden on me and our family. Hardships that neither of us were able to control started to evolve. Though we did the best we could, it seemed there was a point of no return and that time had passed. The stressor's of my disability and a set of events were starting to mount and it was a very gut wrenching period for everyone. I have always believed that things will happen for a reason. Even though some reasons are difficult to understand. What I can share with you is that the girls were very strong and handled things better than could be expected, and I am so proud of them for that. They have adjusted amazingly to this change over the next couple of years. Zoei has gotten nothing but *A*s on her report cards and has been on the high honor roll every quarter since middle school. She is now in eighth grade. Kylee is a straight-A student as well, and she made the high honor roll her first quarter in middle school as a sixth grader. Their mother and I have fifty-fifty shared placement and work together in coparenting, which helps remove much of the tension the girls may feel when sharing their two homes. We make sure they are loved, and we emphasize in no way was this their fault. Again, I am so extremely proud of the way they handled and conducted themselves through that long process, even as young as they were at the time.

While I was waiting for the disability process to work its way through the system, I had tried doing some part-time work. I needed it to be something light in activity and flexible enough to work around my health. I was able to find one position that fit my circumstances, however I eventually had to leave that as well. My disability was eventually processed and awarded to me at the beginning of 2012. I had to depend so much on my family for support, as I had to do in the past. It wasn't easy for me to ask them for help during this. But then again, I had no choice. As before, they were there for me and did everything they possibly could. Never once did anyone complain or look down on me. I had done as much as I could do, and I had worked for as long as I could. I didn't feel that I had anything to be ashamed about anymore. My quality of life is measured by what I can do in the present and in the future, not by what I was able to do in the past. This helps me become productive in other ways. I carefully manage my daily activities, which helps me keep my health in check. I do some volunteering at our elementary school, and some coaching with our local high school girls' varsity softball. I also manage a men's baseball team during the summer months. Most important, I love being the best dad that I can be to the two most precious girls in the world, Zoei and Kylee. I love them dearly!

The girls found this photo and gave it to me for Fathers day in 2011. They put it in a frame where they recorded Happy Fathers Day as a message when I press the button. A very special and thoughtful gift during a difficult time

Disco Cures Cancer – 70's theme; Zoei and I doing the pose

Grandparents Day at Kylee's kindergarten

The girls took dance lessons for several years;
this was taken before their last dance program

The girls and I taking a break walking along a popular
river near our home known as Big Falls

My long time friend and Neurophsycologist taken on the day
of his retirement from the Marshfield Clinic / Hospital

Kylee and I after a baseball game

Kylee after her 6th grade middle school band concert

Zoie after her 8th grade middle school band concert

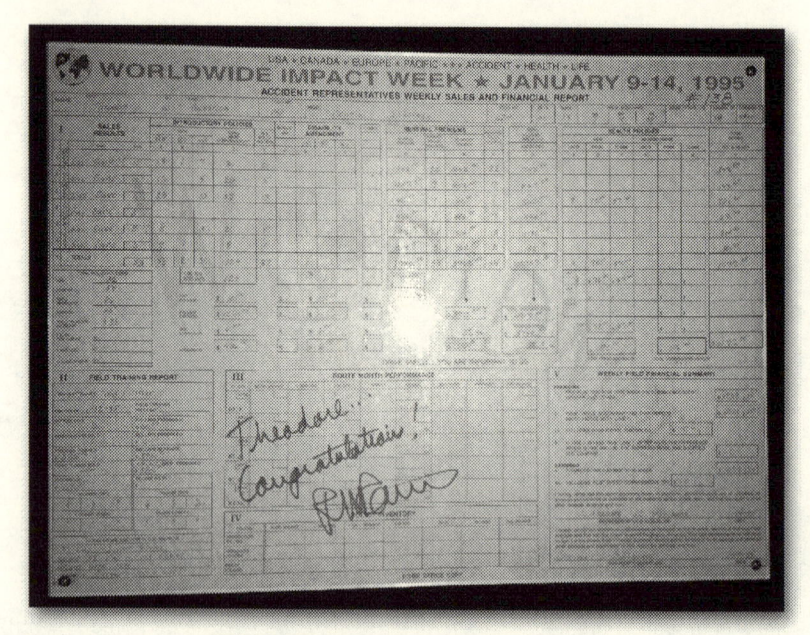

World Wide Impact Award - 1995

The girls and Benny while we were sight seeing in northern Minnesota

After a cross country meet in 2015

Benny, his wife Linda and their two daughters

Benny and Linda at their lake home in Minnesota

Dedication

Over the years, I have had to do a lot of things to make my life as normal as possible and to get back as much as I could through therapy rehabilitation, cognitive rebuilding, brain retraining, medication management, and the long process of natural healing. Then at one point I had to merge everything together, integrating all that I had learned into daily living activities, everyday life experiences, and social interactions. I had an extremely difficult time trying to find my way to fit into this new life and then moving in the direction of getting my career back. It was a very slow, tedious, and unpredictable process. Having to navigate through this with loss of memory made it more difficult and somewhat paralyzing for me because I didn't know how to trust. Throughout my recovery, it was as though I was always walking in the dark. Much of the time I was unsure of the things in front of me or what lay ahead. I had to find that small rainbow to let me know things would be all right. What I needed was a light to help me see where I was going and to guide me through what I couldn't see coming ahead of me. Well, that light for me came in the form of an individual, and his name was Benny Benson. The one trait that I had the most difficulty learning was trust. When I didn't know anyone or remember anything, how was I supposed to truly trust someone to help guide me through something like this?

Benny became my friend when we met at the Mailbu Inn Motel in Medford, Wisconsin, that one evening. What neither of us knew at the time was how large of a role he was going to play in helping me get my new life on track. He did this on every level—personally, socially, individually, and professionally. My sense of pride and personal independence was so important to me, and he became well aware of this. Benny became my friend, my mentor, and my one lifeline to everything that I was attempting to gain back in my life. As I mentioned earlier, outside of my medical circle, he was the only person I had.

My family and so many of my friends have supported me in various ways at various times, and I haven't forgotten any of them or what they did for me. At this particular time, though, there wasn't anyone else who could have done what Benny did.

Trying to work my way back into my career was a job in itself. Doing the social outings and other targeted events were extremely important steps. However, getting back my career also meant getting back my independence, and to me, hopefully that led to getting back a large part of my life. Benny took all of these little pieces I had, which were scattered all over the place, and put them together to make the picture of who and what I am today. He took a personal interest in all of the goals I had set for myself, whether it was the goals that I had about coming back to work with Combined Insurance Company, or the goals I had for learning how to interact with people at a social level. He also took a personal interest in my medical well-being as well. It didn't matter what the topic was or what the challenge was. He always said that if it was important to me, it was important for him. He was there for me twenty-four seven and brought me such a long way through this.

I can never thank him enough for all that he has done for me and all that he will continue to do for me in the future. After all of these years, he is still my only lifeline outside of my medical circle. My daughters have gotten to know Benny and his family well, and we try to see each other as often as we can. We remain in constant contact. I know that I would not be anywhere close to where I am today, and I wouldn't be the person I am today if he hadn't come along at the time he did. As odd as this may sound, I believe this long journey has made me a better man, a better person, a better friend, and a good dad. It has also strengthened my faith. It has taught me to never take anyone or anything for granted, and to live each day as if it was my last. I don't have to accomplish big things; I simply do the very best I can regardless of what that may be. As I said before, I believe God brought Benny into my life when he did because it was part of his plan for me. He knew there was no one else at that particular time that could do this for me, and he knew that I could not do it alone. It is with sincere pleasure, honor, and appreciation that I dedicate this portion of my life's story to my dear friend, Robert "Benny" Benson.

Robert "Benny" Benson as I met him at the Malibu Inn 1991

Printed in the United States
By Bookmasters